TEACH US HOW TO PRAY

Dr. Leon Winslow Crawford, Jr. D.Div

TEACH US HOW TO PRAY
7 Steps of Prayer

Published by:

Kingdom Publishing LLC
1350 Blair Drive, Suite F
Odenton, MD 21113

Printed in the United States of America

ISBN: 978-1-967006-13-7

All scriptural referenced are taken from the King James Version of the Holy Bible.

Cover picture drawn by Lejon Crawford aka *Lejend* and gifted to his father, Dr. Leon W. Crawford at the age of four years old.

TABLE OF CONTENTS

TEACH US HOW TO PRAY

ACKNOWLEDGMENTS

I would like to take this opportunity to recognize and sincerely thank the many people who have taught me, inspired me, prayed for me, and encouraged me throughout the journey of writing this book. This work is not the product of my efforts alone, but the fruit of the wisdom, example, and support poured into my life by others.

First, I extend heartfelt gratitude to my publisher and my brother from another mother, Apostle Antonio M. Palmer. Your guidance, wisdom, and spiritual insight helped me bring this work to completion. Having your leadership and encouragement allowed me to place the final, prayerful touches on this spiritual assignment, and for that I am deeply thankful.

I also want to thank my church family at Citi Praise Church, including all of our leaders and ministers. Thank you for walking with me, supporting me, and faithfully practicing and learning the seven steps of prayer together. Your commitment to prayer made this book not just something I wrote, but something we lived.

A very special thank you goes to Deacon Rodney Cole Williams, whose inspiring push and timely encouragement helped motivate me to complete the final stages of this manuscript. Your words and support came at just the right moment.

To my Priscilla, thank you for being a prayerful and steadfast support. Your faith, encouragement, and intercession strengthened me more than words can express.

I am deeply grateful to my parents, Leon Crawford Sr. and Gail O. Jackson, for their love, foundation, and support throughout my life. Your guidance helped shape the values and faith that made this journey possible.

Finally, as this is my first book, I must acknowledge that I could not have written on the subject of prayer without first witnessing a true lifestyle of prayer lived out daily. That example was found in my grandmother, Willie May Jackson-Lewis. Watching her walk with God, commune with Him, and depend on prayer in real time planted the seed that eventually became this book. Her life was my first lesson in prayer.

To all of you—and to everyone who prayed, encouraged, and believed in me—thank you. This book carries your fingerprints, your prayers, and your love.

FOREWORD

There are moments in the life of the Church when God releases a word that does more than inform — it transforms. It shifts the culture, rekindles devotion, and draws believers into deeper places of intimacy with the Father. Teach Us How to Pray is such a work. It is not merely a book; it is a divine invitation. Dr. Leon Crawford has written a timeless guide that calls the people of God back to the foundation of all spiritual power, all ministry effectiveness, and all authentic Christian living: a life of prayer.

In every generation, God raises up voices who remind the Church of what truly matters. Dr. Crawford is one of those voices. His life, leadership, and ministry have been marked by a consistent devotion to the presence of God. For decades, he has taught, modeled, and lived a prayer-centered walk with Christ. Those who know him personally know that prayer is not a discipline he performs but a lifestyle he embodies. This book flows out of that lived experience— shaped by Scripture, refined by the Spirit, and strengthened through years of shepherding God's people.

What makes Teach Us How to Pray so compelling is its clarity and its depth. Dr. Crawford does not offer formulas or religious clichés. Instead, he leads the reader through seven transformative movements of prayer that are both biblically grounded and spiritually practical. Worship, repentance, the Word, petition, praying in the Spirit, thanksgiving, and obedience—these are not steps, but rhythms. They form the heartbeat of a praying life. Together, they create a pattern of communion that draws the believer into a richer, more authentic relationship with God.

This book reminds us that prayer is not something we master; it is Someone we meet. It is not a religious obligation but a relational invitation. Dr. Crawford writes with pastoral warmth, apostolic authority, and prophetic insight, guiding readers into a prayer life that is vibrant, Spirit-led, and transformative. He shows us that prayer is where identity is affirmed, where destiny is revealed, where bondage is broken, where peace is restored, and where God's power is made manifest.

As you walk through the pages of this book, you will feel the Holy Spirit calling you deeper. You will sense a stirring to return to the secret place, to reignite your devotion, and to recenter your life around the presence of God. You will be challenged, encouraged, and equipped. Most of all, you will be transformed.

My prayer is that every reader who encounters this work will experience a fresh awakening in their spiritual life. May your worship become richer, your repentance more sincere, your petitions more bold, your understanding of the Scriptures more alive, your prayer language more powerful, your gratitude more consistent, and your obedience more immediate. May this book become a companion in your journey, a guide in your formation, and a catalyst for revival in your life.

Dr. Crawford has given the Church a gift—a roadmap back to the heart of God.

Receive this work with expectation, humility, and hunger. Let it shape you. Let it stretch you. Let it draw you closer to the One who still whispers, "Seek My face."

And as you walk this journey, may your heart respond:

"Your face, Lord, will I seek."

— Dr. Antonio M. Palmer, D.Div
Apostolic Leader, Kingdom Alliance of Churches International

PREFACE

Prayer has been the anchor of my life for as long as I have walked with the Lord. It has been the place of my strength, the foundation of my ministry, the well from which I draw wisdom, and the refuge where I have encountered God in the deepest ways. Over the years, through mountain-high victories and valley-low trials, one truth has remained constant: **everything in the Christian life flows from prayer.**

I have seen God heal through prayer.

I have seen God restore families through prayer.

I have seen God open impossible doors, grant supernatural peace, break generational cycles, revive weary hearts, and reveal hidden things—all through prayer.

Yet in all my years of pastoring, mentoring, and teaching, I have also witnessed how many believers struggle to pray consistently or effectively. Some feel unworthy. Others feel unheard. Many simply do not know where to begin. And still others have reduced prayer to a quick ritual—rushed, routine, or reactive—rather than a sacred conversation with the Father.

This book was born from my desire to help believers return to the foundation. To teach prayer the way Jesus taught it. To demystify what has become complicated and restore what has become mechanical. My hope is not just to explain prayer but to awaken prayer in you. To help you discover the rhythm, the joy, the depth, and the power of communion with God.

As I prayed over this project, the Holy Spirit led me to articulate prayer through seven movements: worship, repentance, the Word, petition, praying in the Spirit, thanksgiving, and obedience. These are not formulas but pathways—biblical patterns that form a lifestyle of intimacy with God. Each movement builds upon the other, cultivating a heart that not only speaks to God but listens, responds, and walks in alignment with Him.

This book is written for every believer—whether seasoned in faith or newly walking with Christ—who desires more. More presence. More clarity. More intimacy. More transformation. More of God.

It is written for the intercessor who has grown weary, the disciple who longs for depth, the leader who needs refreshing, the saint who desires answers, and the seeker who wants to know God's heart.

My prayer is that as you turn these pages, your prayer life will shift from ritual to relationship, from duty to delight, from obligation to overflow. I pray you encounter God in ways you never have before. I pray your spiritual hearing becomes sharper, your discernment deeper, your worship richer, your repentance sincere, your petitions bold, your gratitude constant, and your obedience immediate.

Most of all, I pray this book draws you into closer fellowship with the Father who loves you, calls you, embraces you, and invites you into continual communion with Him.

May this book not only teach you how to pray—but empower you to become a person of prayer.

— Dr. Leon Winslow Crawford, Jr.
Senior Pastor of CitiPraise Church

INTRODUCTION

What the Disciples Saw—and Why They Asked the Only Question That Matters

Of all the things the disciples witnessed Jesus do—heal the sick, cast out demons, open blind eyes, confound scholars, multiply food, command storms, and raise the dead — the only thing they ever asked Him to teach them was how to pray. Not once do they ask Him, "Lord, teach us how to preach," or "Teach us how to lead," or "Teach us how to minister." Their singular request reveals a profound truth: the disciples understood that everything Jesus did flowed from His prayer life.

What they observed in Jesus was not simply a man of miracles, but a man of deep communion with the Father. The Gospel writers describe Him repeatedly withdrawing to solitary places to pray (Mark 1:35), praying through the night (Luke 6:12), praying before major decisions (Luke 9:18), praying before miracles (John 11:41–42), praying in agony (Luke 22:44), and praying in triumph (John 17). To walk with Jesus was to witness a life saturated in prayer—not as ritual, but as relationship.

The disciples saw that His strength came from fellowship. His clarity came from communion. His authority came from intimacy. The power that flowed publicly came from the prayer that happened privately. And so, with great humility and even greater hunger, they asked: "Lord, teach us to pray."[1]

Their request must become ours. Prayer is not simply something Christians do; prayer is something Christians become. It forms us, shapes us, reorders us, heals us, breaks us, rebuilds us, and aligns us with the heartbeat of God. Prayer is the language of dependence, the posture of humility, the expression of worship, and the highway of divine power. It is the soul's cry and Heaven's invitation.

Yet many believers struggle with prayer. Some lack consistency. Others lack confidence. Some feel unworthy. Others feel unsure of what to say. Some pray, but feel their prayers stop at the ceiling. Others pray, but sense little intimacy or clarity. Many desire a deeper prayer life—but do not know how to cultivate one.

This book is written for them—and for every believer who longs to pray with greater depth, greater power, and greater intimacy.

Prayer Begins With Knowing How to Approach God

Prayer is more than words. It is approach. It is posture. It is alignment. Scripture teaches that the way we come before God matters. Moses was commanded to remove his sandals before approaching the burning bush[2]; Isaiah cried out that he was a man of unclean lips when he beheld the Lord[3]; David declared that he would enter God's house "in the multitude of Thy mercy" (Psalm 5:7). Prayer requires reverence because prayer invites us into the presence of the Holy One.

This is why Jesus did not begin His model prayer with request, but with worship: "Our Father, who art in heaven, hallowed be Thy name." Worship is not the warm-up to prayer—it is the entryway. It shifts the heart, clears the mind, and places us in the proper posture before we present our petitions. As one scholar notes, worship reorients the entire inner world toward God before a single request is made.[4]

The Purpose of This Book

This book is designed to take believers step by step into a life of meaningful, Spirit-filled prayer. It will guide you through the foundational movements of prayer—worship, repentance, the Word, petition, praying in the Spirit, thanksgiving, and action—not as isolated techniques but as a unified spiritual rhythm. These are not formulas; they are pathways. They shape the heart, align the will, and ignite the spirit.

Each chapter will take you deeper into the nature and purpose of prayer. You will learn how to cultivate a consistent prayer life, how to identify hindrances that block spiritual flow, how to persevere when prayer feels dry, how to recognize God's responses, and how to operate in a lifestyle of ongoing communion with the Father. By the end, you will not merely understand prayer—you will be formed by it.

Prayer Is Relationship, Not Ritual

True prayer is not defined by eloquence, length, or routine. It is defined by relationship. Jesus did not die so that people could recite formulas; He died to restore fellowship between God and humanity. Prayer is the language of that restored fellowship. When you pray, you are not speaking into the air. You are entering the throne room of grace with confidence (Hebrews 4:16). You are engaging the One who loves you, hears you, and responds to you.

That response may not always look like what you expect—but God always answers. Sometimes the answer is yes. Sometimes it is no. Sometimes it is wait. Sometimes it is direction. Sometimes it is peace. Sometimes it is an inner transformation that becomes the answer before circumstances ever shift. But prayer always produces movement. Something always changes—either in the situation or in your soul.

A Journey That Will Change You

As you walk through the chapters of this book, you may find:
Your desire for prayer increasing.
Your awareness of God's presence deepening.
Your spiritual confidence strengthening.
Your understanding of Scripture expanding.
Your communion with the Holy Spirit becoming more natural.

Your heart growing more tender and more aligned with the Father's will.

This is the natural result of a life given to prayer. For prayer does not simply change circumstances—prayer changes you. It bends your will into His. It refines your motives. It awakens your spirit. It stabilizes your emotions. It purifies your intentions. It transforms your perspective. Prayer is the furnace in which God forms the soul of His servant.

If you embrace the principles in these pages, prayer will cease to feel like an obligation and become an encounter. It will shift from duty to delight, from strain to intimacy, from self-effort to Spirit-led communion. You will discover what the disciples discovered: that the power of Jesus was the fruit of His prayer life—and that the same power becomes available to those who learn how to pray the way He prayed.

A Final Word Before We Begin

This book is not meant to be read once and shelved. It is meant to be practiced. It is meant to be lived. It is meant to shape your daily walk with God. My prayer for you is the same request the disciples uttered to Jesus:

"Lord, teach us to pray."

May this journey lead you into deeper communion, greater clarity, stronger faith, and a more intimate walk with the Father.

May your prayer life become the most powerful, fruitful, and transformative dimension of your Christian experience. And may every chapter draw you closer to the heart of the One who created you, loves you, hears you, and invites you continually into His presence.

Footnotes

1. Luke 11:1 (KJV)
2. Exodus 3:5 (KJV)
3. Isaiah 6:5 (KJV)
4. See commentary on Matthew 6:9 in various biblical scholarship, including The Holy Bible: King James Version (Nashville: Thomas Nelson, 1982).

WORSHIP

"Worship is the soul's recognition of God's worth." — A.W. Tozer

"Enter into his gates with thanksgiving, and into his courts with praise: be thankful unto him and bless his name"— Psalms 100:4

Entering His Presence the Right Way

Prayer begins with worship because worship is the God-ordained doorway into His presence. Scripture directs us clearly: "Enter His gates with thanksgiving, and His courts with praise."[1] Thanksgiving is not merely a polite gesture or a religious courtesy—it is the spiritual key that opens the gate. Praise is the step that carries us deeper into the courts of the King. Worship, therefore, is not the warm-up to prayer; it is the opening movement of prayer itself.

Worship is not defined by a slow song, raised hands, or goosebumps. It is an intentional posture of the heart—one that approaches God with reverence, affection, awe, and surrender. Worship acknowledges God's unmatched worth. Before a believer ever asks God for anything, the worshiper gives God what He desires most: the offering of the heart. This is why worship always precedes effective prayer.

Worship as Holy Approach

Throughout Scripture, God makes clear that how we approach Him matters. When Moses encountered the burning bush, he was instructed to remove his sandals because he stood on holy ground.[2] The command was not about footwear—it was about posture. Holy ground demands holy approach. Similarly, when David danced before the ark of God with "all his might" (2 Samuel 6:14), he demonstrated that worship is not tied to dignity, but to devotion.

5

The structure of the tabernacle in Israel's worship reinforces this idea vividly. Worshipers did not begin in the Holy of Holies. They began at the gate—with praise. They advanced into the courts through thanksgiving. Only through consecration and reverence could they draw near to God's presence. The entire system taught Israel that worship is the singular pathway into divine encounter.[3]

Even Jesus followed this divine pattern. When teaching His disciples how to pray, He began not with requests but with worship: "Our Father in heaven, hallowed be Your name." By placing worship at the front of prayer, Jesus revealed that communion with God begins in reverence.[4]

Many believers today struggle in prayer not because God is distant, but because they skip the step that aligns their spirit with His presence. Worship clears the mind, softens the heart, awakens faith, and prepares the believer for meaningful communion.

The Meaning of Worship

To understand worship biblically, we must examine the words Scripture uses to describe it. The primary Hebrew word translated "worship" is *šāchâ*, meaning "to bow down, prostrate oneself, or show reverence."[5] The primary Greek word in the New Testament is *proskuneō*, which carries the same meaning: "to fall or kneel before one in reverence or submission."[6] Worship, then, is not passive. It is voluntary surrender. It is an intentional lowering of the self in order to lift up the Sovereign God. This is why we were taught that prayer should be done from your knees, even from childhood we started praying by the side of our beds on our knees. This was the first sign of reverence and worship.

Another meaning for worship (which is my personal favorite) *sabāh,* meaning deep feelings of adoration expressed openly before God. Worship is not a performance—it is your feelings displayed toward God.

When you pray, surrender both your body and emotions to this moment of intimacy. Worship matters to God because it is not about you praying to get what you want—it's about offering Him what *He* wants.

It's also not about throwing up a few cold, careless "Hallelujahs" or "Thank You, Jesus" then jumping straight into bargaining and begging.

Don't do that.

Plan to take your time and genuinely love on God.

Clear your mind of your wants and begin to:

- thank Him,
- praise Him,
- and adore Him for who He is.

Adore Him because He is God.

Therefore, HEARTFELT participation is a MUST—not in the sense of physical theatrics only, but in the offering of one's soul. When worship is genuine, the heart responds: hands lift naturally, tears fall freely, voices soften or rise, and the soul feels the nearness of God. These responses are not emotional manipulation; they are the natural expression of a heart touched by divine presence.

True worship flows from a reverent heart—not a routine. It is not a recitation of memorized phrases. It is the deliberate turning of the heart toward God with honor and affection. As one Christian scholar summarized: "Worship is the believer's response of all that they are —mind, emotions, will, and body—to all that God is."[7]

Worship Involves Emotion—Because God Gave Us Emotion

Some Christians mistakenly believe emotions are unspiritual. Yet Scripture teaches the opposite. God promises to replace the "heart of stone" with a "heart of flesh" (Ezekiel 36:26), meaning a heart that is tender, responsive, and alive. Jesus affirmed this truth when He said worship must be offered "in spirit and in truth" (John 4:24). Spirit speaks to sincerity and internal posture; truth speaks to authenticity and alignment with God's nature. Neither excludes emotion.[8]

The God who created emotion is not offended when affection rises in worship. If relationships, art, or achievements can move our hearts, surely the presence of God should move us even more. What God rejects is empty emotionalism divorced from truth; what He receives is sincere affection flowing from reverence.

Religion can create a spiritual callous—a "stony heart."

But Ezekiel 36:26 says:

"A new heart also will I give you… I will take away the stony heart and give you a heart of flesh."

That means feelings matter to God.

Even in the New Testament, worship still triggers something in God. John 4:24 says:

"God is a Spirit, and they that worship Him must worship Him in spirit and in truth."

The Greek word for "spirit" is pneuma, meaning breath, wind, or the human soul—the same breath God breathed into Adam, making him a living soul with emotions and feelings.

And God desires those emotions from us—the same passion we show at ball games, concerts, or community events.

In Matthew 15:22–28, the Canaanite woman cried out for Jesus to heal her daughter. Her cry got the disciples' attention—but not Jesus'.

But verse 25 says:

"Then came she and worshipped Him…"

And that is what moved Jesus.

Her worship carried her request into the heart of God.

Signs You Have Entered True Worship

True worship is not measured by outward noise or visible expression; it is measured by the sense of divine nearness. A person may worship quietly and yet be deeply aware of God's presence. Another may lift hands or cry tears because the weight of glory touches their inner life.

The authentic indicators of worship include softened hearts, quieted minds, heightened spiritual awareness, and a deepened sense of intimacy. In worship moments, believers often describe feeling God's peace resting on them, His love washing through them, or His Spirit stirring within them. These experiences cannot be manufactured; they are evidence that Heaven has drawn near.

Worship Is Not Performance — It Is Relationship

Worship is not about skill, talent, poetic phrasing, or musical excellence. God is not moved by the performance of worship — He is moved by the sincerity of the worshiper. A worship song may be technically excellent yet spiritually empty. Conversely, a simple, unpolished expression of honor may be profoundly pleasing to God.

A father treasures his child's simple drawing because of the love behind it, not the artistic technique. In the same way, worship becomes precious to God when it flows from a sincere heart. What matters is not the impressiveness of the offering but the authenticity of the heart presenting it.

A Story About Real Value

Several years ago, my wife and I purchased a piece of art that was expected to increase in value over time. We stored it carefully, waiting for the right frame. It was an intentional investment—measured, preserved, and protected.

Around that same time, on a Sunday while I was preaching, my young son—only four years old—sat quietly and drew a picture of me. When we arrived home, he handed it to me, his eyes full of excitement, and said, "Daddy, I drew a picture of my hero. I want to grow up and be just like you."

In that moment, my heart melted. I picked him up, hugged him, kissed him, and spoke words of affirmation over his life. I didn't wait to find a frame. I hung that drawing up immediately—and to this day, it remains on my wall.

That drawing may have cost less than a dollar to make, but to me, it is priceless. Its value was not found in its material worth, but in the heart from which it was given. It touched my heart because it came from his heart. *(The book cover is that very same picture by Lejon Crawford)*

This is the essence of worship. Worship is not about external worth or polished presentation; it is about the offering of the heart. When we worship, we give God what is most valuable to Him—ourselves.

What Happens When We Skip Worship

When believers move too quickly into prayer—jumping straight into requests, needs, and petitions—their prayer life becomes transactional rather than relational. Prayer loses intimacy when worship is absent. Worship is not a preliminary step; it is spiritual alignment. It prepares the heart to pray in faith, not fear; in confidence, not desperation.

Skipping worship is like trying to enter a home without using the key. The door remains closed. The heart remains restless. The distractions remain loud. Worship stills the noise. It anchors the soul. It opens the spiritual door.

Worship Is for God—Not for Us

While worship profoundly benefits the believer, its primary purpose is not self-help—it is honor. Worship is about giving God what He alone deserves. Ironically, it is in giving God what He desires that we receive what we need. Worship positions us under the flow of God's peace, presence, wisdom, and strength. But we receive these not because we demanded them, but because we honored Him.

Worship Breaks Religion Off the Soul

Religion approaches God formally, mechanically, and without affection. Worship breaks the shell of religion by awakening sincerity. Religion performs; worship surrenders. Religion recites; worship responds. Religion numbs; worship revives. When worship becomes lifestyle rather than ritual, the heart becomes tender, the spirit becomes sensitive, and prayer becomes intimate.

Worship Transforms You

Worship reshapes the inner person. It softens pride, quiets anxiety, elevates faith, heals wounds, and restores spiritual clarity. Worship changes the worshiper. It realigns priorities, purifies motives, and strengthens identity. Most importantly, worship makes you hungry—not for blessings, but for God Himself.

The more you worship, the more you begin to desire the Giver over the gifts. This is the ultimate purpose of worship—not merely to prepare you for prayer, but to transform you into a person who delights in the presence of God.

Concluding Exhortation

Begin every moment of prayer with worship. Let your first words honor Him, not request from Him. Let your heart bow before your mouth speaks. Worship is the door. Worship is the posture. Worship is the first step into the throne room of grace.

When you start with worship, you do not approach God as a beggar—you approach Him as a beloved child entering the presence of a loving Father.

Footnotes

1. Psalm 100:4 (KJV)
2. Exodus 3:5 (KJV)
3. See discussions on tabernacle worship and divine approach in biblical scholarship; cf. The Holy Bible: King James Version (Nashville: Thomas Nelson, 1982).
4. Matthew 6:9 (KJV)
5. *"Definition of Worship,"* GotQuestions Ministries, accessed January 2025, https://www.gotquestions.org/definition-of-worship.html.
6. Greek lexicon entry for *proskuneō*, BibleHub Lexicon, accessed January 2025, https://biblehub.com/lexicon/john/4-24.htm.
7. *"Definition of Worship,"* GotQuestions Ministries.
8. Ibid

REPENTANCE

"Create in me a clean heart, O God." — Psalm 51:10

Cleansing the Heart So Prayer Can Flow

It's important to have a clean heart when coming into the presence of a holy God.

Our conscience is the battleground where Satan attacks us, using thoughts of:

- guilt,
- shame,
- and condemnation.

How many times have you tried to pray, and suddenly old memories, past sins, random thoughts, or distractions storm your mind? That's not a coincidence; that is exactly where the enemy aims—because guilt has worked on mankind since the beginning of time, which has made man run from God instead of feeling the boldness to run to God.

As an example:

After Adam and Eve sinned, the first thing they did was hide.

They covered themselves with fig leaves and avoided God's voice out of fear, shame, and condemnation.

But here's what bothered me about their story:

There were no Ten Commandments.

No 613 laws.

Only one rule in one garden.

Yet after breaking that single command, guilt made them run from God instead of running to Him—and people still respond the same way today.

Most Christians focus on the sin, not the promise.

On their failure, not God's grace.

On their guilt, not God's garden.

Because of this, many believers avoid prayer, or they try to "perform" their way into God's acceptance.

But condemnation has **never** come from Christ.

Romans 8:1 says:

"There is therefore now no condemnation to them which are in Christ Jesus…"

Condemnation is not God's voice—it is the voice that tries to keep you *away* from God's presence.

If worship opens the door into God's presence, repentance prepares the heart to remain there. Worship draws you into proximity — repentance grants you purity. Together, the two form the foundation of every meaningful prayer life. Where worship lifts the soul in reverence, repentance humbles it in honesty. Worship exalts God; repentance exposes the self. Worship focuses upward; repentance looks inward. And both are necessary if prayer is to be powerful, intimate, and transformative.

Repentance is not merely an apology; it is a spiritual cleansing. It is the deliberate act of turning away from sin and turning the heart toward God with sincerity. It is the moment when the believer acknowledges truthfully, "Lord, this area of my life is misaligned with Your will, and I cannot fix it apart from Your grace." Repentance is not self-condemnation but Spirit-led acknowledgement. It is not religious shame; it is relational honesty. And Scripture makes it clear:

God responds to honesty far more quickly than He responds to eloquence.

Why Guilt Kills Prayer

Romans 8:6 says: "To be carnally minded is death, but to be spiritually minded is life and peace." If Satan can keep your mind on guilt, shame, and failure, then he knows you won't step into the Spirit—and God moves in the Spirit. He also knows that if he can keep you condemned, your prayers will carry death, not faith. Many prayers die before they leave your mouth because they're wrapped in guilt instead of grace. But Hebrews 4:16 invites us to: "Come boldly unto the throne of grace..." Boldness doesn't come from being perfect—it comes from being forgiven.

Why Repentance Matters to Prayer

In Psalm 66:18, the psalmist makes a sobering statement: "If I regard iniquity in my heart, the Lord will not hear me."[1] This does not mean that God suddenly becomes deaf or indifferent, but that sin — especially unconfessed sin — disrupts the clarity of the relationship. Just as static disrupts a radio signal, sin disrupts the flow of prayer. Many believers pray earnestly yet feel as if their prayers are hindered, not because God refuses to answer, but because the heart refuses to surrender.

Isaiah echoes this reality when he writes, "Your iniquities have separated between you and your God, and your sins have hid His face from you."[2] Once again, Scripture reveals that the problem is not divine distance but human uncleanliness. Repentance restores what sin has interrupted. It realigns the heart with God's holiness and reopens the line of communication.

This is why repentance must occur before meaningful petition. When the heart is weighed down with guilt, bitterness, secrecy, or spiritual clutter, the believer will struggle to pray with confidence.

But when the heart has been cleansed through repentance, boldness returns—the confidence that God hears, God responds, and God forgives.

The apostle John assures believers of this truth: "If we confess our sins, He is faithful and just to forgive us our sins, and to cleanse us from all unrighteousness."[3] Repentance is not merely God forgiving the sin—it is God cleansing the stain, removing the weight, and restoring the soul to purity.

Repentance as Relational, Not Ritual

It is important to understand that repentance is not a ritualistic act but a relational response. God is not interested in mechanical apologies or repeated phrases that have no intention behind them. The Hebrew word most closely associated with repentance, šûb, means "to turn back, to return, to restore."[4] It pictures a person changing direction, not merely changing vocabulary.

In the New Testament, the Greek word metanoeō means "to change one's mind"—not simply to regret behavior, but to rethink, re-evaluate, and reverse internal posture.[5] Thus, repentance is both directional and transformational. It is a return to God and a reformation of self.

God honors repentance because repentance honors God. When the believer approaches Him with a truthful heart—not hiding, not excusing, not blaming—God's mercy flows freely. David demonstrated this beautifully when he cried, "Create in me a clean heart, O God, and renew a right spirit within me."[6] He was not asking for a second chance; he was asking for a clean heart. David understood that repentance is not about revisiting sin but about restoring communion.

Some believers avoid repentance because they associate it with condemnation. But Scripture makes a crucial distinction: the Holy

Spirit convicts—Satan condemns. Conviction draws you back to God; condemnation pushes you away. Conviction says, "You are better than this; come home." Condemnation says, "You are worthless; stay in the shadows." Repentance is always Spirit-led, never shame-driven.

How Repentance Changes the Inner Life

When a believer repents sincerely, several changes take place within the soul. First, the conscience is cleansed. Guilt loses its grip, and the believer no longer feels the weight of spiritual heaviness. The mind becomes clearer, free from the nagging sense of hiddenness or unworthiness. Confidence in prayer grows, because the believer knows that nothing stands between them and God.

Second, repentance softens the heart. Sin hardens; repentance tenderizes. Many believers find they cannot enter into worship deeply or hear God clearly because their hearts have become spiritually calloused. Repentance removes the callousness. It re-sensitizes the soul to the movements of the Spirit. A tender heart is the ideal environment for prayer.

Third, repentance restores spiritual authority. When sin remains unchecked, it weakens the believer's spiritual strength. But when repentance is practiced, authority returns. The believer stands in prayer with a renewed sense of boldness, clarity, and spiritual sharpness.

Fourth, repentance strengthens humility. Pride resists God, but humility attracts Him.[7] Repentance keeps the believer grounded, aware of their dependence on the Father, and conscious of their need for grace. It is impossible to walk in humility and not walk in repentance. The two grow together.

Repentance Must Be Daily

Just as we wash our bodies daily, the heart must be cleansed regularly. Repentance is not something reserved for major spiritual failures; it is a daily spiritual hygiene. Jesus taught this principle when He washed the disciples' feet. Peter resisted, but Jesus replied, "He who has bathed needs only to wash his feet to be entirely clean."[8] In other words: "Your salvation cleansed you, but your daily walk requires continual cleansing."

Daily repentance protects the believer from subtle sins—attitudes, motives, hidden pride, lingering resentment, coldness of heart, careless words, or unexamined thoughts. Often, it is not the great sins that disrupt prayer but the small ones—the ones we overlook. Repentance brings even the smallest matters before God so that nothing interferes with communion.

Repentance Must Be Specific

General repentance—"Lord, forgive me of my sins"—is often a sign that the believer is not being honest with themselves. True repentance names the sin, confronts the motive, and surrenders it to God. When David said, "Against You, and You alone, have I sinned,"[9] he acknowledged both the act and the motive. He took responsibility. Repentance cannot heal what we refuse to confront.

Repentance Brings Freedom

One of the most immediate fruits of repentance is freedom. Many believers live with spiritual heaviness because they have unconfessed sin lingering in the heart. The moment they repent, that heaviness lifts. Peace enters. Joy rises. Hope awakens.

Repentance frees the believer from guilt, frees the spirit from oppression, frees the conscience from weight, and frees the heart from anguish. It is not punishment—it is liberation.

Repentance Restores Fellowship

The goal of repentance is not simply to remove sin; it is to restore fellowship. God is a relational Father who desires closeness with

His children. Sin breaks fellowship—not sonship, but closeness. Repentance restores that closeness. John assures us: "If we walk in the light…we have fellowship with one another, and the blood of Jesus cleanses us from all sin."[10]

When the believer walks in transparency before God, intimacy deepens. Prayer becomes more natural, more joyful, and more powerful. Repentance transforms prayer from a struggle into a privilege.

A Heart Postured for Repentance

A repentant heart is a humble heart, a teachable heart, a submitted heart. It is a heart that invites the Holy Spirit to search its inner rooms, illuminate hidden areas, and bring correction. Repentance is not a one-time act but a continual posture—one that says, "Lord, if there is anything in me that misrepresents You, reveal it and cleanse it."

This posture protects the believer from self-righteousness. It guards against spiritual stagnation. It keeps the soul alive, tender, and responsive. It makes the believer moldable—and God shapes moldable hearts more easily than rigid ones.

A Childhood Lesson I Never Forgot

When I was around seven years old, my father bought my Christmas gifts and hid them in his closet. I was told, *"Stay out of that closet."*

Well…curiosity said otherwise.

One day he sent me into his room to grab something,

and when I saw a blanket bulging from the closet shelf,

I did what any young boy might have done —

I peeked.

And man, did I peek.

There they were—all my Christmas toys.

And just like that, I realized Santa wasn't real.

Excited and nervous, I hurried out and handed my father the item he asked for.

Then he asked:

"Son... did you look in my closet?"

"No, Dad," I said—knowing full well I had lied.

Later that evening, we sat down to watch my favorite TV show, *The Courtship of Eddie's Father.*

I can still hear the theme song:

"People let me tell you 'bout my best friend..."

But this episode was about honesty.

As the show played, guilt filled my little heart.

It was so heavy I began to cry.

My father looked at me and said:

"Son...what's wrong?"

I burst out sobbing and crying and with a repenting voice I said:

"I looked at my toys! I'm sorry, Daddy! I lied!"

My father sighed gently and said,

"Well... looks like I'm going to have to take them all back."

But at that moment,

I didn't care about the toys —

I cared about the relationship.

I cared more about disappointing my father

than losing what he bought me for Christmas.

He talked with me about honesty,

told me he loved me,

kissed me on the forehead,

and tucked me into bed.

I slept like a baby that night.

And to my surprise on Christmas morning —

he never took the gifts back. Everything I asked for was under the tree.

That was the greatest Christmas of my life.

Repentance Works Just Like That

Repentance is being honest with your Heavenly Father.

It is coming clean so Satan cannot fill your heart with guilt.

When you confess your sins, God removes:

- shame,
- guilt,
- fear,
- and condemnation.

1 John 1:9 says:

"If we confess our sins, He is faithful and just to forgive us… and to cleanse us."

Faithful means He can be counted on.

Just means He is righteous in doing it.

Cleanse means He wipes away everything that stood between you and Him.

Friend, God wants me to tell you something:

He will not take His GIFTS back when you repent.

In fact—He will release more to your life.

This can become one of the best seasons you've ever had in your life if you learn to come before God with honesty and a clean heart and as you read this I declare that it will be your best.

Conclusion: Cleansed Hearts Carry Powerful Prayers

Repentance is not a detour on the way to prayer—it is the way. It prepares the atmosphere, cleanses the conscience, and creates room for God's presence to dwell. A repentant believer prays differently—with boldness, humility, confidence, and clarity. Nothing clogs the spiritual pipeline. Nothing weighs the conscience down. Nothing interferes with the flow of the Spirit.

Make repentance a daily practice. Invite the Holy Spirit to reveal anything that hinders your communion with God. Allow Him to cleanse the heart, renew the mind, and restore the soul. For it is the cleansed heart that carries the cleanest, clearest, and most effective prayers.

Footnotes

1. Psalm 66:18 (KJV)
2. Isaiah 59:2 (KJV)
3. 1 John 1:9 (KJV)
4. See Hebrew definition for *šûb* in standard Old Testament lexicons; cf. Strong's Concordance, entry H7725.
5. See Greek definition for metanoeō in Strong's Concordance, entry G3340.
6. Psalm 51:10 (KJV)
7. James 4:6 (KJV)
8. John 13:10 (KJV)
9. Psalm 51:4 (KJV)
10. 1 John 1:7 (KJV)

THE WORD

"The Word is God's contract between God and man, so know what
the word says about the word."
—Dr. Leon W. Crawford

"The Word will not return back to Him empty"—Isaiah 55:11

This step in prayer is when you remind God of His Word — not
because He forgets what He said, but because speaking His Word
aligns both the spiritual realm and the earth realm with His promises.

When God spoke "Let there be," the earth responded to His voice.
And the earth still recognizes God's voice today.

So when you pray, understanding what God says about His Word
gives you access to something supernatural—something powerful—
something unshakable.

God's Word Will Not Return Empty

Isaiah 55:11 tells us God's Word:

- will not return void,
- will not come back empty,
- but will accomplish what God sends it to do.

God's Word is not weak.

God's Word does not fail.

God's Word does not expire.

When we pray we must understand Gods word is a contract written
to man, and man must know what the contract says so we should

remind God what he said about his word! your prayer becomes more than emotion — it becomes divine language that give you rights to ask him for anything that lines up with his will.

HIS WILL IS HIS WORD AND HIS WORD IS THE CONTRACT

WHAT DID HE SAY IN HIS CONTRACT?

HIS WORD is A Lamp for Direction

Psalm 119:105 says:

"Thy word is a lamp unto my feet and a light unto my path."

When this verse was written, a nighttime traveler in the desert carried a lamp for two reasons:

1. to illuminate the road ahead,
2. and to reveal snakes hidden in the path.

God's Word still does both today:

- It lights the way to a better path.
- It exposes the snakes — anything in your past, present, or even certain people who might hinder your journey.

His Word is not just information — it is illumination and revelation.

HIS WORD PROMISES TO STAND THE TEST OF TIME

Isaiah 40:8 —- *the grass withereth, the flower fadeth: but the word of our God shall stand for ever.*

Why Many Christians Struggle in Prayer

Many believers talk to the grace side of God—the side that grants mercy—but not directly to God Himself, because they are not speaking His language.

Prayer is a language-based exchange.

If I speak English and you speak French, both of us could be sincere—but the conversation would still break down.

It is the same way spiritually.

God speaks two fluent languages:

1. **His Word** (Scripture),
2. **and tongues** (the language of the Spirit).

Most Christians pray "feel good" or emotional prayers—and God hears them because of His grace—but they are not praying the language of Heaven.

That's why sometimes there is a disconnect.

Why God Says, "Remind Me of My Word"

Isaiah 43:26 says:

"Put Me in remembrance…"
God isn't forgetful.
He doesn't need reminders.
We need them.
And the spirit realm needs them.
And our own heart needs them.

When you pray God's Word, you are declaring:

- His authority
- His promises
- His covenant
- His will
- His truth
- His language

Speaking Scripture is not quoting poetry—it is placing God's contract back on Heaven's desk.

The Word as a Contract God Cannot Break

Hebrews 4:12 says:

"The Word of God is living, powerful, sharper than any two-edged sword…"

Jesus Himself said:

"Heaven and earth shall pass away, but My words shall not pass away." — Matthew 24:35

God's Word is His contract, sealed by His nature.

And God cannot break His own Word.

Just as business deals require both parties to read and agree on the terms, God requires us to:

- read His Word,
- understand it,
- believe it,
- and pray it.

Agreement gives you access.

Faith activates that access.

The Word guarantees the outcome.

Pray the Word — The True Language of God

To pray God's Word, you must speak it—not emotionally, not traditionally—but scripturally.

Praying Scripture and Aligning With the Voice of God

If worship opens the door and repentance cleanses the heart, then the Word of God becomes the foundation upon which all effective prayer is built. Prayer without Scripture is like a ship without a compass—passionate but directionless, sincere but unstable, active but easily misled. When believers anchor their prayers in God's Word, they anchor their lives in God's voice. Scripture is the language of Heaven, the vocabulary of divine truth, and the instrument through which the Spirit shapes, strengthens, and directs the soul.

Many Christians attempt to pray from emotion alone, hoping sincerity will compensate for lack of alignment. But sincerity is never a substitute for truth. Emotion fluctuates, desire drifts, and human perspective shifts with seasons—but the Word of God stands fixed, eternal, unchanging. Jesus declared, "Heaven and earth shall pass away, but my words shall not pass away."[1] When believers pray according to Scripture, they pray prayers that cannot decay, weaken, or expire.

The Word as God's Breath in Written Form

The Bible describes itself as "God-breathed," meaning that Scripture originates from the very breath of God.[2] When a believer prays Scripture, they are not merely speaking text—they are echoing the breath of the Almighty. They are returning God's words back to Him in faith. The prophet Isaiah reveals a profound truth about the divine nature of Scripture: "So shall my word be that goeth forth out of my mouth: it shall not return unto me void."[3] This means God's Word always accomplishes what He sends it to do. It is active, powerful, self-fulfilling.

Because Scripture is God's voice in written form, praying Scripture ensures we never pray outside His will. Too often, believers ask God for things He never promised, then grow discouraged when they do not receive them. Scripture brings clarity and alignment. It shapes our desires into God's desires, our requests into His intentions. Jesus taught plainly: "If ye abide in me, and my words abide in you, ye shall ask what ye will, and it shall be done unto you."[4] To have His Word abiding in us is to pray with divine authorization.

The Word Reveals God's Heart, Nature, and Will

It is impossible to know God without knowing His Word. The Scriptures are not merely a book; they are revelation—the unveiling of God's character, desires, promises, warnings, and ways. The Bible reveals what God loves, what He hates, what He values, and what He blesses. Without the Word, believers pray blindly, guessing at God's intentions instead of praying with conviction.

The Word reveals God's nature. He is holy, just, merciful, loving, patient, sovereign, and faithful. When believers pray according to His nature, they pray prayers consistent with who He is. For instance, God cannot bless wrongdoing, endorse bitterness, deny justice, or contradict His holiness. But He delights in mercy, responds to humility, strengthens righteousness, honors faith, and protects the oppressed. Scripture becomes the lens that keeps believers from forming a false image of God—one shaped by culture, emotion, or tradition rather than by truth.

The Word Is a Weapon in Prayer

Prayer is not only communion; it is also conflict. The believer faces spiritual opposition, and Scripture becomes the primary weapon in spiritual warfare. Paul describes the Word of God as the "sword of the Spirit,"[5] the only offensive weapon listed in the armor of God. Jesus Himself modelled this truth during His temptation in the wilderness. Each time Satan presented a lie, Jesus responded with, "It is written."[6] He did not respond with emotion, opinion, or personal logic—He responded with Scripture.

If the Son of God used Scripture as His weapon, then believers must do the same. When the enemy whispers fear, believers declare God's promise of peace. When the enemy hurls accusations, they declare God's affirmation. When darkness threatens identity, Scripture restores confidence. When temptation rises, Scripture provides the escape. The Word is not passive; it is confrontational. It dismantles lies, breaks strongholds, and exposes deception.

The Word Strengthens Faith for Prayer

Faith is not formed by willpower or optimism. Faith is birthed by hearing God's Word. Paul writes, "Faith cometh by hearing, and hearing by the Word of God."[7] When believers read, meditate on, or declare Scripture, their faith is nourished. This is why spiritually weak seasons often coincide with seasons when believers neglect the Word.

Scripture works like oxygen to the spirit. It revives, strengthens, and stabilizes. It transforms hope into conviction and longing into expectation. Without Scripture, faith becomes fragile—too fragile to sustain a life of prayer. But with Scripture, faith becomes fortified, steady, and resilient. A believer saturated with the Word prays differently—with greater boldness, clarity, and confidence.

The Word Guides Prayer and Prevents Error

Many believers unintentionally pray outside the will of God because they have not learned to let Scripture shape their requests. They pray according to emotion rather than revelation. They ask God to bless relationships He already warned against, to revive things He intends to remove, or to provide resources He has not assigned to their purpose. Scripture protects believers from misguided prayers.

For example, praying for revenge violates the command to love enemies.[8] Praying for God to overlook sin contradicts His holiness.[9] Praying for God to endorse bitterness, pride, jealousy, or selfish ambition places the believer in opposition to His nature.

But when prayer is shaped by Scripture—"Thy will be done"—the believer prays not from impulse but from instruction.

The Word Illuminates the Mind and Directs the Spirit

David proclaimed, *"Thy word is a lamp unto my feet, and a light unto my path."*[10] Scripture illuminates dark places—not only in the world, but in the heart. It reveals motives, corrects attitudes, exposes deception, and clarifies direction. When believers pray without the Word, they may operate from confusion. But when they pray with the Word, they walk in illumination.

The Word also teaches believers how to perceive God's voice. The more familiar they become with Scripture, the easier it becomes to discern the Spirit's whisper. Scripture becomes the standard by which believers test impressions, dreams, promptings, and prophetic words. The Spirit never contradicts the Word He authored.

The Word Transforms the Inner Life

Scripture is not simply something we read — it is something that reads us. Hebrews describes God's Word as "living and active... discerning the thoughts and intents of the heart."[11] The Word penetrates. It convicts. It transforms. It reshapes identity, reforms habits, renews thinking, and reshapes character.

Many believers pray for transformation yet struggle to grow because the Word has not yet reshaped their inner world. Prayer may invite God to work, but Scripture gives God the tools to perform the work. Without the Word, transformation is slow and shallow. With the Word, transformation becomes deep and enduring.

The Word Must Be Spoken, Not Only Read

Scripture is most powerful when it is declared. Jesus spoke Scripture to Satan. The prophets spoke Scripture to nations. Believers must speak Scripture to their circumstances, families, emotions, and bodies. Speaking the Word reinforces it in the mind, anchors it in the heart, and releases it into the atmosphere with authority.

When you declare the Word, you are not trying to convince God; you are aligning yourself with Him. You are reminding your soul of God's truth, resisting the enemy's lies, and releasing divine authority into your situation.

The Word and the Spirit Work Together

Some believers emphasize Scripture but neglect the Spirit; others emphasize the Spirit but neglect Scripture. But the two are inseparable. Jesus declared that His words "are spirit, and they are life."[12] The Spirit empowers the Word, and the Word clarifies the Spirit. Together, they bring balance, depth, revelation, and discernment.

A prayer life rooted in Scripture and ignited by the Spirit becomes unshakeable.

Conclusion: Stand on What God Has Spoken

Prayer becomes powerful when it stands on what God has already said. Scripture is the foundation that stabilizes every request. It transforms prayer from hopeful wishing into confident petition. When believers pray the Word, they pray Heaven's language. They speak God's promises back to the God who made them. They stand on truth that cannot be revoked. They anchor their souls in revelation that cannot be shaken.

To grow in prayer, grow in the Word. To increase spiritual authority, anchor yourself in Scripture. To strengthen your faith, feed it with divine truth. And to hear God more clearly, immerse yourself in His written voice.

For it is the Word of God that gives prayer its power, purpose, and precision.

Footnotes

1. Matthew 24:35 (KJV)
2. 2 Timothy 3:16 (KJV)
3. Isaiah 55:11 (KJV)
4. John 15:7 (KJV)
5. Ephesians 6:17 (KJV)
6. Matthew 4:1–11 (KJV)
7. Romans 10:17 (KJV)
8. Matthew 5:44 (KJV)
9. Hebrews 12:14 (KJV)
10. Psalm 119:105 (KJV)
11. Hebrews 4:12 (KJV)
12. John 6:63 (KJV)

STEP 4
PETITION

"And this is the confidence that we have in him, that, if we ask anything according to his will, he heareth us: and if we know that he hear us, whatsoever we ask, we know that we have the petitions that we desired of him." — 1 John 5:14-15

Petitioning God is another important step in prayer—one that must be done correctly, not out of fear, confusion, or desperation. The Bible makes it clear:

1. Ask anything according to His will, He will hear you
2. If you know He hears you, then you also know you already have the petition you asked for.

This is not my opinion; it is Scripture.

His Will Is His Word

1 John 5 says we must ask "according to His will."
But how do you know His will?

It's simple:

His will is His Word. God's will is not hidden. It is not mysterious. It is not complicated. It is written plainly in Scripture. So when you pray God's Word, you are praying directly in alignment with His will — and that is why He hears you.

God Hears His Word Better Than Emotional Prayers

Many Christians pray emotional prayers, traditional prayers, denominational prayers (Baptist, Pentecostal, Catholic, Methodist styles), "soft" prayers, or silent prayers.

Now, God hears all kinds of prayers because He is full of grace. But the prayers that move Heaven the fastest are the ones filled with His Word, not just our feelings. When God hears His Word in your mouth, He responds because His Word is eternal, unchanging, legally binding, and spiritually powerful.

God's Word Is a Petition—a Formal Request to the Highest Authority

The dictionary defines a petition as "a formal written request appealing to authority with respect to a particular cause." That is exactly what happens when you pray Scripture.

When you pray God's Word it becomes a formal request, written in Heaven long before you prayed it on Earth, and it goes directly to the One with all power and all authority.

The One who can turn a no into a yes.
The One who can open a door no man can shut.
The One who listens when no one else can help.

That is why John writes "If we know that He hears us… we *know* we have the petition we desired of Him."

He didn't say you might have it. He said you have it.

Pray God's Word Over What You're Believing For

As you read this book, I want you to think about the things you are believing God for:

- a healing?
- a breakthrough?
- a job or new opportunity?
- a restored relationship?
- wisdom for your next season?
- provision for your household?
- deliverance from something that has held you back?

Whatever it is —
start praying God's Word over it now.

I sense even as I write this that God is near.
His presence is close.
He is listening.
He is ready.
And He is standing there waiting
to honor His Word in your life.

Prayer Activation: Petition

Speak this out loud:

"Father, according to Your Word, I present my request before You. Let it be done according to Your will. I know You hear me—and I know I have what I asked, because You promised it in Scripture."

Stand on it. Believe it. Expect it. Asking According to God's Will and Standing on His Promises

Once worship has carried you into God's presence, repentance has cleansed your heart, and the Word has aligned your spirit with His truth, the believer is now properly prepared to bring petitions before the Lord. Petition—the act of asking God for what is needed or desired—is one of the most familiar expressions of prayer, yet it is also among the most misunderstood. For many Christians, prayer begins with asking, but biblically, asking comes after worship, repentance, and alignment with Scripture. Only when the heart is rightly postured can petition become powerful, effective, and fruitful.

Petition is not begging. It is not pleading with uncertainty. It is not approaching God as if He were reluctant or resistant. Petition is a bold act of faith rooted in relationship. It is the confident presentation of requests to a Father who loves His children, hears His people, and delights in responding. Jesus Himself declared, "Ask, and it shall be given you; seek, and ye shall find; knock, and it shall be opened

35

unto you."[1] Petition is not only permitted by God—it is invited, encouraged, and expected.

Petition as a Covenant Expression

What makes petition so powerful is that it is based on covenant. Believers do not approach God merely as distant subjects addressing a sovereign monarch; they approach Him as covenant sons and daughters speaking to their Father. The foundation of this confidence is not personal merit but divine promise. John affirms this when he writes, "This is the confidence that we have in Him, that, if we ask anything according to His will, He heareth us."[2]

Petition, therefore, is covenantal. It stands on what God has already revealed, already promised, and already made available. Petition is not the attempt to persuade God; it is the act of agreeing with God. It is aligning earthly requests with heavenly intention.

Jesus reinforced this covenant dynamic when He said, "What things soever ye desire, when ye pray, believe that ye receive them, and ye shall have them."[3] Petition is a covenant privilege—the right of the believer to bring their desires before the Father with assurance.

Petition Requires Alignment With God's Will

The apostle John's instruction is clear: God hears the prayer that is "according to His will." How does a believer discern God's will? Through His Word, His character, and the leading of the Spirit. Petition becomes powerful when the believer asks not from impulse, fear, desperation, or selfish ambition, but from alignment.

To pray outside of God's will is to pray outside of God's promise. But to pray according to His will is to pray with divine authority. Many believers struggle with unanswered petitions because their requests do not flow from alignment. They request things God never promised, never purposed, or never intended for their season. The will of God is not an obstacle to answered prayer; it is the foundation of answered prayer.

Jesus demonstrated this in Gethsemane when He prayed, *"Not my will, but Thine be done."[4] This was not resignation—it was alignment. Petition is powerful when surrendered to divine wisdom.

Petition Must Flow From a Clean Heart

Jesus taught that a believer's petitions are affected by the condition of their heart. After commanding His followers to "believe" when they pray, He immediately added, "And when ye stand praying, forgive."[5] Forgiveness and petition are linked. The heart cannot hold bitterness while expecting blessing. Petition requires purity. A grudge becomes a barrier; resentment becomes interference. Petition must flow from a heart free of offense.

Repentance prepares the heart for petition by removing guilt, shame, and clutter. Forgiveness keeps the heart clear of barriers. Humility ensures the heart remains open to God's leading. Petition from a clean heart carries spiritual weight.

Petition Is Not Passive—It Is an Act of Faith

When believers petition God, they must do so with faith. Petition is not simply speaking to God; it is believing God. Jesus commanded, "When ye pray, believe that ye receive them."[6] Faith is the engine of petition—without it, requests become empty words.

Faith-driven petition is active. It looks for God's movement. It expects divine intervention. It refuses to let fear, doubt, or discouragement dilute the request. Petition is not timid; it is bold. The writer of Hebrews urges believers to come to the throne of grace with confidence (Hebrews 4:16). Petition is the exercise of that confidence.

To petition God without faith is to speak without expectation. To petition God with faith is to speak with certainty grounded in His character.

Petition Must Be Specific

General prayers often reflect general faith. When Jesus encountered the blind man outside Jericho, He asked, "What wilt thou that I should do unto thee?"[7] Although the man's condition was obvious, Jesus required specificity. Specific petitions reveal thoughtful faith. They demonstrate clarity of desire and focus of expectation.

Vague petitions often reveal an internal uncertainty about what the believer desires or expects. Specific petitions reveal a heart aligned and confident. They allow the believer to recognize God's answer clearly when it arrives.

A specific petition is not merely, "Lord, bless me," but, "Lord, grant me wisdom for this decision," or "Heal this wound," or "Open this door," or "Provide this resource." Specificity strengthens gratitude when the answer comes.

Petition and Persistence

Some petitions are answered immediately; others require persistence. Jesus taught this repeatedly. In the parable of the persistent widow, the unjust judge granted her request because she refused to stop asking (Luke 18:1–8). If persistence moved an unjust judge, how much more will it move a righteous Father?

Persistence is not begging—it is commitment. It is the ongoing declaration of faith. It is the refusal to surrender hope. Persistence shapes the believer as much as it shapes the outcome.

Daniel prayed for three weeks before breakthrough came, not because God delayed, but because spiritual warfare resisted the answer.[8] Persistence pushes through resistance. Some prayers are delayed not by divine withholding but by spiritual conflict. Petition must be relentless when the Spirit compels perseverance.

Petition Is Not Manipulation

Petition must never be used as a tool of manipulation. God cannot be coerced by tears, bargains, rituals, or emotional pressure. He responds to faith, not manipulation. Petition is not a negotiation; it is communion. It is the expression of trust, not control.

Believers must guard against praying from selfish ambition or flesh-driven desire. James warns, "Ye ask, and receive not, because ye ask amiss, that ye may consume it upon your lusts."[9] Petition outside of God's nature and will is prayer without power.

Petition Must Be Accompanied by Obedience

Petition opens the door; obedience walks through it. Many believers pray for outcomes they are unwilling to participate in. They pray for financial blessing but resist stewardship. They pray for healing but refuse forgiveness. They pray for opportunities but avoid preparation. Petition is powerful, but its fullness requires obedience.

When God gives instruction—even simple instruction—it becomes part of the answer. The man with the withered hand was healed when he obeyed the command, "Stretch forth thy hand."[10] Petition invites divine intervention; obedience activates it.

Petition Anchored in Scripture

The most effective petitions are Scripture-based petitions. When believers pray according to God's promises, they pray with divine authority. Scripture supplies language when emotions fail. It provides clarity when circumstances confuse. It strengthens faith when doubt arises.

A Scripture-based petition sounds like:

"Lord, You promised to supply all my need—I stand on that promise."

"Father, You said wisdom is given liberally—I ask for it now."

"God, You declared that by Your stripes we are healed—I declare that healing."

These petitions do not manipulate God; they honor Him by trusting His word.

Conclusion: Ask, Because Your Father Listens

Petition is the joyful privilege of every believer. It is the moment in prayer when the child speaks to the Father, not with timidity but with trust. It is an act of faith, dependence, and alignment. When petition flows from worship, repentance, Scripture, and faith, it carries divine power.

Do not be afraid to ask. Do not be hesitant to present your desires, fears, needs, and longings before God. He invites your petition. He receives your request. And He responds—in His wisdom, in His timing, and in His love.

When you pray according to His will, you pray according to His heart. And the heart of God delights in answering the cries of His children.

Footnotes

1. Matthew 7:7 (KJV).
2. 1 John 5:14 (KJV).
3. Mark 11:24 (KJV).
4. Luke 22:42 (KJV).
5. Mark 11:25 (KJV).
6. Mark 11:24 (KJV).
7. Mark 10:51 (KJV).
8. Daniel 10:12–13 (KJV).
9. James 4:3 (KJV).
10. Mark 3:5 (KJV).

TEACH US HOW TO PRAY

CHAPTER 5

PRAYING IN THE SPIRIT

"The Spirit Himself maketh intercession for us." — Romans 8:26

Praying in the Holy Spirit—praying in tongues—is one of the most powerful steps in prayer. Yet it is also one of the most misunderstood, misjudged, and underused gifts in the Body of Christ. Tongues is not emotional hype. It is not showing off. It is not "Pentecostal noise." Tongues is a spiritual language given by God for supernatural communication between your spirit and His.

What the Bible Actually Says About Tongues

Let's look carefully at Scripture:

1 Corinthians 14:2
"For he that speaketh in an unknown tongue speaketh not unto men, but unto God: for no man understandeth him; howbeit in the spirit he speaketh mysteries."

This alone tells us two things:
1. Tongues is not a human language—it is a God-language.
2. Tongues carries mysteries—truths your spirit knows but your mind cannot explain.

1 Corinthians 14:14
"For if I pray in an unknown tongue, my spirit prayeth, but my understanding is unfruitful."

Tongues bypasses the limitations of your natural understanding. Your spirit does the praying while your mind takes a step back. This is why praying in the Spirit is so powerful—it allows God to pray through you.

Tongues Is a Language Satan Cannot Decode

This may shock some people, but it is biblical truth: Satan cannot understand tongues. He cannot interpret this language. He cannot translate it. He cannot intercept it. Tongues locks the devil out of the conversation between you and God.

No wonder the enemy has spent generations spreading fear, confusion, and false teaching around tongues. If he can keep Christians from praying in the Spirit, he keeps them from:

- building their faith,
- receiving direct mysteries from God,
- praying the perfect will of God,
- and tearing down spiritual strongholds.

Jude 20 says:

"Building up yourselves on your most holy faith, praying in the Holy Ghost."

Tongues builds you up —
and tears the enemy down.

Why So Many Christians Fear Tongues

Let's be honest; many believers have been scared away from tongues because of miseducation, judgment from others, denominational bias, or fear of "doing it wrong." But tongues is a gift from God, not a badge of spiritual superiority. The enemy has done a good job spreading confusion and division around this gift because he knows its power. If Christians truly understood tongues, the enemy's strategies against them would collapse overnight.

Language Has Always Been a Spiritual Battleground

To understand tongues correctly, you must understand the power of language in Scripture.

In Genesis 11, at the Tower of Babel, the people had:

- One language
- One speech
- One mind

And because of this unity, they began building a tower toward Heaven. Their goal was wrong, but their unity was powerful. God said something astonishing in Genesis 11:6, *"This people is one, and they all have one language... and now nothing will be restrained from them which they have imagined to do."* This shows us something spiritual:

Language determines access, power, and what Heaven or Hell can or cannot do.

So God confused their language because they were united in the wrong purpose just like in Genesis 11 the people was scattered throughout the earth.

But notice this; in Acts 2, God reversed the Tower of Babel—not through confusion, but through Holy Ghost tongues. This is where the people language was changed for the purpose of speading the gospel with words and miracles. So, as we pray in the Holy Ghost or speaking in tongues we receive power and authority for the purpose of God.

Acts 2 — The Heavenly Language Returned

At Pentecost, they were in one place, on one accord, and had one expectation. Suddenly, a sound from Heaven filled the room, and cloven tongues—split tongues of fire—rested on each person. The word cloven refers to something parted or divided (like the split hoof of clean animals in Israel's diet). Spiritually, this symbolizes separation. When you pray in tongues, you separate yourself from earthly thinking, earthly language, earthly doubt, and earthly limitations.

Tongues is Heaven's way of giving you a higher language for a higher conversation.

Tongues Is the Gateway to Deeper Prayer

When you pray in the Holy Spirit:

- your faith rises
- your inner man strengthens
- your confusion lifts
- your fear breaks
- and your spirit becomes sensitive to God's voice.

Praying in tongues is pure Spirit-to-Spirit communion—no middleman, no interference, and no misunderstanding. It is the perfect prayer offered through the perfect Spirit to the perfect God.

Prayer Activation: Pray in the Spirit

If you are filled with the Holy Spirit, then take a moment to:

Speak softly. Pray in tongues. Let the language flow like a river rising inside of you.

If you have not yet received this gift, then pray with an open heart:

"Holy Spirit, fill me. Give me utterance. Release Your heavenly language in me. Teach my spirit to pray beyond my understanding." Let Him come. Let Him flow. Let Him pray through you.

Partnering With the Holy Spirit in Supernatural Intercession

Among the most powerful dimensions of prayer is the ability to pray in the Spirit. Worship brings you into God's presence, repentance purifies the heart, the Word aligns the mind, and petition engages the Father with faith—but praying in the Spirit draws the believer into a supernatural partnership with God Himself. It is prayer beyond intellect, beyond emotion, beyond the limitations of human vocabulary. It is prayer flowing from the Holy Spirit through the believer, empowering them to intercede, to war, to build, to strengthen, and to align with Heaven's agenda.

Many believers stop at praying with their understanding—using natural language shaped by their thoughts, desires, and needs. But Scripture reveals a deeper realm of communion where the Holy Spirit takes the lead, where the believer yields their tongue, will, and heart to divine influence. Paul writes, "For if I pray in an unknown tongue, my spirit prayeth, but my understanding is unfruitful."[1] This does not diminish understanding; it simply means the mind becomes secondary while the spirit takes the forefront.

What It Means to Pray in the Spirit

Biblically, praying in the Spirit refers both to praying by the empowerment of the Holy Spirit and to praying in tongues as the Spirit gives utterance. Paul affirms both dimensions. He instructs believers to "pray with the spirit, and…pray with the understanding also."[2] Jude later urges the church to "build yourselves up on your most holy faith, praying in the Holy Ghost."[3] Praying in the Spirit, then, includes:

- Allowing the Holy Spirit to inspire and direct natural-language prayer
- Yielding to the Spirit in supernatural prayer (tongues)
- Entering a Spirit-led flow where the believer becomes an instrument of divine intercession

Tongues are not a sign of spiritual superiority—they are a gift of divine assistance. They allow believers to pray with accuracy when they lack understanding, to intercede when they lack knowledge, and to align with God when they lack clarity.

Why Praying in the Spirit Is Necessary

There are moments when believers simply do not know what to pray. The human mind cannot always comprehend the depths of a situation—the emotional complexity, the unseen warfare, the divine will at stake. In those moments, the Spirit Himself intervenes. Paul writes: "Likewise the Spirit also helpeth our infirmities: for we know not what we should pray for as we ought."[4] The phrase "helpeth our infirmities" means "to take hold of together with us"—the Spirit becomes our partner in prayer.

Paul continues: "But the Spirit Himself maketh intercession for us with groanings which cannot be uttered."[5] These groanings are not human emotions but divine communication—expressions from the Spirit that bypass human limitation. When believers pray in the Spirit, they enter a realm where their words no longer originate from their intellect but from the Holy Ghost, who intercedes according to the will of God (Romans 8:27).

Praying in the Spirit Builds the Inner Man

Jude tells believers that praying in the Holy Ghost builds you up on your most holy faith.[6] The Greek word translated "build up" is epoikodomeō, meaning "to construct, fortify, or strengthen from the inside out."[7] Praying in the Spirit fortifies the believer's faith, stabilizes the emotions, renews the mind, and strengthens spiritual resolve.

Many Christians suffer unnecessary spiritual weakness because they rely solely on natural prayer. But spiritual warfare demands spiritual strength. Praying in the Spirit develops endurance, resilience, and sensitivity to God's presence. It strengthens the believer in ways human language cannot.

Praying in the Spirit Produces Clarity

The Spirit not only intercedes—He illuminates. As believers pray in the Spirit, revelation often flows. Thoughts become clearer. Discernment sharpens. Scripture opens with new insight. Confusion lifts. Wisdom emerges. This is because the Spirit of God "searches all things, yea, the deep things of God" (1 Corinthians 2:10). Spiritual clarity is not produced by intellectual striving but by spiritual communion.

At times, a believer may begin a prayer burden without understanding its purpose. But as they pray in the Spirit, God reveals the matter—perhaps a person needing intercession, a spiritual attack needing resistance, or a divine instruction needing obedience. Praying in the Spirit aligns the believer with Heaven's perspective.

Praying in the Spirit Protects Against Spiritual Attacks

Paul identifies tongues as a weapon of spiritual warfare. He writes that praying in tongues is a way God equips the believer for spiritual battle (Ephesians 6:18). When believers pray in the Spirit, they pray beyond the level the enemy can fully interpret, intercept, or withstand. Praying in the Spirit disrupts demonic strategy, confuses the enemy's communication, and strengthens the believer's resistance to temptation, fear, and discouragement.

Many breakthroughs occur only after believers shift from natural prayer into Spirit-led prayer. The enemy can resist human effort, but he cannot withstand Holy Ghost intercession. When the Spirit begins to groan through the believer, spiritual atmospheres shift, strongholds crumble, and obstacles lose their power.

Praying in the Spirit Creates Alignment

Praying in the Spirit aligns the believer's heart with the will of God. Paul writes that the Spirit "intercedes for the saints according to the will of God."[8] There are moments when the believer's desires conflict with God's intentions. Natural prayer may pull in one direction, but Spirit-led prayer pulls the heart into alignment.

Over time, praying in the Spirit refines motives, transforms desires, and reshapes the internal world. The believer begins to desire what God desires, love what God loves, resist what God resists, and pursue what God wills. The Spirit does not merely intercede through the believer—He intercedes in the believer, transforming the inner life.

Praying in the Spirit Releases Breakthrough

In Acts 4, when the early church prayed, the place was shaken—not because of eloquence, but because of spiritual power. In Acts 16, Paul and Silas prayed and worshiped in prison, and the foundations shook, chains broke, and doors opened. Breakthrough is rarely a product of natural prayer alone. It is produced when Heaven touches earth through Spirit-led intercession.

Believers often face situations requiring more than ordinary prayer—strongholds in families, generational patterns, demonic interference, emotional wounds, spiritual confusion, financial resistance, relational conflict. Praying in the Spirit reaches deeper than natural words can reach. It targets roots, not symptoms. It operates with divine accuracy.

Many breakthroughs remain locked because believers stop praying prematurely. But when they shift into praying in the Spirit, they tap into an unending supply of strength, wisdom, and divine power. Spirit-led prayer continues long after natural vocabulary fades.

Praying in the Spirit Produces Rest

Isaiah prophesied that God would speak to His people through "stammering lips and another tongue," saying, "This is the rest... this is the refreshing."[9] Praying in the Spirit brings supernatural rest

—rest from anxiety, rest from striving, rest from emotional turmoil. The Spirit intercedes not only for needs but for the soul itself.

Stress drains the heart. But praying in the Spirit restores equilibrium. The believer emerges from Spirit-led prayer calmer, clearer, lighter, and more grounded. This is because praying in tongues engages the spirit while bypassing the mind, which is often the source of exhaustion.

Praying in the Spirit Is for All Believers

Some church traditions suggest that praying in tongues is a gift reserved for a select few. But Scripture makes clear that praying in the Spirit is available to all who receive the Holy Ghost. On the Day of Pentecost, "all were filled with the Holy Ghost and began to speak in other tongues."[10] Peter later declared that the promise is for "you, your children, and all who are afar off."[11] Paul even said, "I would that ye all spake with tongues."[12] While the public gift of tongues requires interpretation, the private prayer language is for every Spirit-filled believer.

Praying in the Spirit Must Be Practiced

Like any spiritual discipline, believers grow stronger in this grace the more they practice it. Praying in the Spirit should not be occasional or reserved for crisis. It should be a daily rhythm, a consistent flow. Paul wrote, "I thank my God, I speak with tongues more than ye all."[13] His effectiveness in ministry was deeply connected to his prayer life in the Spirit.

The more believers pray in the Spirit, the more sensitive they become to God's leading, the more discerning they become in spiritual matters, and the more powerful they become in spiritual warfare. Praying in the Spirit is spiritual exercise—it builds strength, endurance, and power.

Conclusion: Partner With the Spirit Who Prays in You

Praying in the Spirit is one of the greatest gifts God has given His people. It is Heaven praying through humanity, the Spirit joining with the believer to accomplish divine purposes. It is a supernatural language of intimacy, warfare, revelation, and transformation.

Do not limit your prayer life to the capacity of your mind. Pray beyond yourself. Yield to the Holy Ghost. Let Him intercede. Let Him groan. Let Him guide. Let Him strengthen. For when you pray in the Spirit, you do not pray alone—you pray with God Himself praying through you.

Footnotes

1. 1 Corinthians 14:14 (KJV)
2. 1 Corinthians 14:15 (KJV)
3. Jude 20 (KJV)
4. Romans 8:26 (KJV)
5. Ibid
6. 1 Corinthians 14:4 (KJV)
7. See Greek definition of *epoikodomeō* in Strong's Concordance, entry G2026.
8. Romans 8:27 (KJV)
9. Isaiah 28:11–12 (KJV)
10. Acts 2:4 (KJV)
11. Acts 2:39 (KJV)
12. 1 Corinthians 14:5 (KJV)
13. 1 Corinthians 14:18 (KJV)

CHAPTER 6
THANKSGIVING

"Give thanks unto the Lord; for he is good: because his mercy endureth for ever" — Psalms 118:1

The Posture That Attracts God's Presence and Unlocks His Peace

Thanksgiving is one of the most powerful, transformative, and often overlooked dimensions of prayer. While worship focuses on who God is and petition asks for what God promises, thanksgiving responds to what God has already done. It is the spiritual discipline of remembering, acknowledging, and celebrating the goodness of the Lord. But thanksgiving is far more than polite gratitude—it is a posture of faith, a declaration of trust, and a weapon of spiritual warfare. It shifts the atmosphere of the heart. It aligns the soul with God's nature. It opens doors, breaks heaviness, and draws the believer deeper into intimacy with God.

Thanksgiving is commanded throughout Scripture. Paul writes, "In every thing give thanks: for this is the will of God in Christ Jesus concerning you."[1] This does not mean we thank God for all things but that we thank Him in all things. Thanksgiving is not dependent on circumstance; it is dependent on covenant. Gratitude is not based on what we feel; it is based on what we know—that God is good, God is faithful, God is present, and God is working even when we cannot yet see the full picture.

Thanksgiving as a Spiritual Posture

Thanksgiving is not simply an action—it is a posture. It is the orientation of the heart toward God in humility, remembrance, and trust. David exemplifies this posture when he declares, "I will bless the LORD at all times: His praise shall continually be in my mouth."[2] Continually means without interruption. Thanksgiving becomes the rhythm of the believer's life, not a seasonal response but a daily practice.

A thankful heart is a sensitive heart, a humble heart, a worshipful heart. Gratitude shifts the believer's perspective from what is lacking to what God has supplied, from what is painful to what God has promised, from what is uncertain to what God has spoken. Thanksgiving strengthens faith by recalling God's faithfulness in the past. It is the deliberate act of remembering that if God did it before, He can do it again.

Thanksgiving Honors God

Thanksgiving is not merely a gesture of politeness toward God—it is a declaration of His worth. When a believer offers thanksgiving, they are acknowledging God as the source of every blessing, every provision, every breakthrough, every breath. James explains this principle, writing, "Every good gift and every perfect gift is from above, and cometh down from the Father of lights."[3] Thanksgiving honors God as the giver of gifts, the sustainer of life, and the author of every blessing.

In Luke 17, Jesus heals ten lepers, yet only one returns to give thanks. Jesus asks the piercing question: "Were there not ten cleansed? But where are the nine?"[4] This account reveals that thanksgiving is noticed by Heaven. Gratitude distinguishes believers who are near to God from those who merely receive from Him. The one who returned received more than healing—he received wholeness. Thanksgiving does not merely acknowledge what God has done; it positions the believer to receive even more.

Thanksgiving Releases Peace

One of the greatest blessings linked to thanksgiving is supernatural peace. Paul teaches, "Be careful for nothing; but in every thing by prayer and supplication with thanksgiving let your requests be made known unto God."[5] The result of combining prayer and thanksgiving is profound: "And the peace of God, which passeth all understanding, shall keep your hearts and minds through Christ Jesus."[6]

Thanksgiving guards the heart and mind. It acts like a spiritual shield against anxiety, worry, and fear. The believer who gives thanks is less shaken by circumstances because gratitude anchors them in God's character. Thanksgiving shifts the internal atmosphere until peace overrules panic. Even before the answer comes, peace arrives—because thanksgiving acknowledges that God is already at work.

Thanksgiving Strengthens Faith

Every time a believer thanks God for past blessings, their faith for future answers is strengthened. Gratitude rehearses God's faithfulness. It replays the miracles, provisions, victories, healings, protections, and moments of divine intervention. Thanksgiving is memory in motion—the recollection of what God has done. David practiced this when he faced Goliath. He remembered the lion and the bear, and that memory fortified his faith for the giant.[7]

Thanksgiving refuses to let the soul forget the goodness of God. It dismantles doubt by anchoring the heart in truth. When a believer says, "Lord, I thank You for what You have done," they are simultaneously declaring, "Lord, I trust You for what You will do." Gratitude is faith expressed in past tense.

Thanksgiving Breaks Spiritual Heaviness

Scripture reveals that thanksgiving is a spiritual weapon against heaviness. Isaiah prophesies of the Messiah giving God's people "the garment of praise for the spirit of heaviness."[8] Gratitude is that garment. Thanksgiving lifts the soul when darkness tries to settle. Depression weakens under praise. Anxiety dissolves under gratitude. Oppression loses its grip when thanksgiving rises.

Many believers struggle with heaviness because they have not learned to clothe themselves with thanksgiving. Instead of rehearsing problems, they must rehearse God's goodness. Instead of magnifying fears, they must magnify the Lord. Thanksgiving shifts the emotional climate—it brings light into dark places, joy into weary hearts, and hope into discouraged minds.

Thanksgiving Opens Doors in the Spirit

Thanksgiving is one of the ways believers access the presence of God. The psalmist writes, *"Enter into His gates with thanksgiving, and into His courts with praise."[9] Thanksgiving opens the gate. Praise takes the believer into the court. Worship brings them before the throne. No believer enters God's presence accidentally—thanksgiving is part of the divine protocol.

When gratitude flows freely, spiritual doors open easily. Revelation increases. Sensitivity to the Holy Spirit sharpens. The believer enters dimensions that remain closed to the unthankful. Thanksgiving is not a ritual; it is a key.

Thanksgiving Attracts Multiplication

Thanksgiving releases multiplication. In John 6, Jesus took the five loaves and two fish, and before performing the miracle, He gave thanks.[10] After thanksgiving, the bread multiplied. Gratitude precedes increase. This is a spiritual principle woven throughout Scripture: what you thank God for, He multiplies. What you complain about, He minimizes. Complaining shrinks faith; thanksgiving expands it.

When believers thank God for small provisions, He entrusts them with greater ones. When they thank Him for their current season, He prepares them for the next. Thanksgiving invites God to multiply His work in the believer's life.

Thanksgiving Purifies Motives

Gratitude softens the heart and keeps motives pure. When believers continually give thanks, they remain aware of God's grace. Humility deepens. Entitlement dissolves. Thanksgiving protects the believer from pride—for how can one boast when everything is recognized as a gift?

A thankful believer is a humble believer, and Scripture teaches that God gives grace to the humble.[11] Gratitude keeps the believer in a posture where they can receive more grace, more strength, more revelation, and more anointing.

Thanksgiving Is an Act of Obedience

Thanksgiving is not optional—it is commanded. The psalmist writes, "O give thanks unto the LORD; for He is good."[12] Gratitude is obedience rooted in revelation. The believer gives thanks not because circumstances are ideal, but because God is good. His goodness does not fluctuate with seasons. His character remains constant.

Even Jesus modeled thanksgiving. Before raising Lazarus, He prayed, "Father, I thank thee that thou hast heard me."[13] Before performing miracles, He gave thanks.[14] If the Son of God practiced thanksgiving, His followers must do likewise.

Thanksgiving Produces Joy

Joy is the natural fruit of gratitude. Thanksgiving magnifies the joy of salvation, strengthens emotional resilience, and awakens hope. When believers thank God continually, they cultivate joy internally. It is difficult for despair to rule a thankful heart. Gratitude shifts perspective until joy springs forth.

Paul could rejoice in prison because gratitude kept his heart free. Thanksgiving does not deny hardship; it transcends it. It lifts the believer above circumstances into the steadiness of God's presence.

Thanksgiving Must Be a Lifestyle

Biblical thanksgiving is not seasonal or occasional. It is continual—a lifestyle. Paul urges believers to give thanks "always for all things."[15] Thanksgiving becomes the ongoing conversation between the believer and God. It marks their waking moments, shapes their prayers, and fills their worship.

A thankful believer is sensitive to blessings others overlook—a sunrise, protection, provision, friendships, healing, daily mercies, unexpected kindnesses. Thanksgiving refines the believer's vision until they see God's fingerprints everywhere.

Conclusion: Thanksgiving Transforms Everything It Touches

Thanksgiving is one of the most transformative disciplines in the Christian life. It shifts atmospheres, deepens intimacy, strengthens faith, and draws the believer closer to the heart of God. It opens gates, releases peace, dismantles heaviness, and invites divine multiplication. Thanksgiving is not merely something believers do—it is who they become.

Let thanksgiving shape your prayer life. Let gratitude influence every request, every season, every circumstance. Thanksgiving will anchor your soul in God's goodness, empower your spirit with His peace, and elevate your heart into continual fellowship with Him.

For the believer who lives in thanksgiving lives in the presence of God. Thank Him in advance even before you see the manifestation of your prayer being answered. THANK HIM BY FAITH!

Footnotes

1. 1 Thessalonians 5:18 (KJV).
2. Psalm 34:1 (KJV).
3. James 1:17 (KJV).
4. Luke 17:11–19 (KJV).
5. Philippians 4:6 (KJV).
6. Philippians 4:7 (KJV).
7. 1 Samuel 17:34–37 (KJV).
8. Isaiah 61:3 (KJV).
9. Psalm 100:4 (KJV).
10. John 6:11 (KJV).
11. James 4:6 (KJV).
12. Psalm 107:1 (KJV).
13. John 11:41 (KJV).
14. Matthew 15:36 (KJV).
15. Ephesians 5:20 (KJV).

TEACH US HOW TO PRAY

CHAPTER 7
ACT ON IT!

Even so faith, if it hath not works, is dead, being alone"
— James 2:17

Never ask God for anything you are not willing to go after. Prayer without movement is incomplete. Faith without action is powerless We must understand that faith is an action word. You cannot pray for a blessing and sit still. You cannot ask God to open a door while refusing to knock. You cannot pray for increase while being afraid to step out. Prayer may start the process, but action finishes it.

Faith Must Be Demonstrated

The old saints used to say, "If you take one step, God will take two." The meaning of this saying is that God responds to movement. If you refuse to move, you limit what faith can produce.

A body without a spirit is dead. The Bible teaches that faith without deeds is the same way—useless and ineffective. Genuine faith transforms your mindset and your lifestyle.

Faith produces action:

- love,
- kindness,
- service,
- obedience,
- courage,
- boldness,
- and decisive steps.

Simply *saying* you have faith means nothing without steps to prove it. Works cannot get you into Heaven, but works can bring Heaven into your situation.

Serving Others Activates Faith

One of the fastest ways to stir your faith is to help hurting people Serving others aligns you with God's heart. Mission trips, soup kitchens, homeless shelters, nonprofit work—all of these activate faith through compassion. Faith grows when you move beyond yourself. Faith matures when you step into purpose. Faith strengthens when you bless others. Your spirit will never feel at its best until you help someone who cannot repay you.

Actions That Reveal Faith

Beyond serving, faith shows itself through practical steps:

If you pray for a job:
Submit the application — and go talk to someone in the company.

If you pray for a new residence:
Go look at the place. Schedule a tour. Walk the property.

If you pray for a loan:
Meet with the bank manager. Fill out the paperwork.

If you pray for ministry opportunities:
Talk to your leader. Share your plan. Move forward boldly.

If you pray for deliverance:
Remove access points, change habits, seek accountability.

If you pray for healing:
Act like recovery has begun. Speak the Word. Take steps of faith.

Fear cannot lead you. Doubt cannot guide you. Timidity cannot be your shepherd. Action is the evidence that you believe God heard you.

Your Answer Is Already There—Go After It

If you've made it this far in the book, it tells me something—You want your prayers answered, you desire results, and you are hungry for more of God. So let me tell you something many believers never hear: Your prayers have already been answered, but you haven't moved on them yet. God has prepared opportunities, relationships, open doors, and resources, but now it's time for you to confront what's stopping you.

- Go look.
- Go ask.
- Go touch.
- Go step.
- Go believe.
- Go seize what God has placed in front of you.

The Cruise Ship Story

I once heard a story about two men on a cruise ship. They met each other often, and one man noticed the other bringing food to his cabin every night. The first man assumed he must be wealthy to afford all that food.

On the last day, as the ship prepared to dock, he asked, "How did you afford all those meals?" The man looked confused and said, "Afford them? I'm not rich. Those meals were free—they came with the ticket."

The man could have eaten every day, but he didn't realize the food was already included. Many believers are living just like that man— praying for things that God has already provided, but never stepping out to receive them or never leaving the cabin to go after it.

Biblical Examples of Faith in Motion

Peter walking on water (Matthew 14:29): He stepped out before the water became stable.

The four lepers (2 Kings 7): They said, "Why sit we here until we die?" And when they moved, God caused the enemy army to

63

flee, leaving behind wealth, food, and provision. When you move, Heaven moves.

Prayer Activation: Action

Ask yourself:

"What is one step I can take today that agrees with what I prayed?"

Then do it. Not tomorrow, not next year, but today, because God has prepared more than enough for you—so much that you will have to share the blessing. But you must go after it. GO FOR IT TODAY!!

Prayer Does Not End With Amen—It Begins With ACTION

Prayer is not complete when the believer says "Amen." In many ways, prayer truly begins at that moment. After worship has aligned the heart, repentance has cleansed the soul, the Word has shaped understanding, petition has expressed desire, praying in the Spirit has strengthened faith, and thanksgiving has cultivated gratitude—the final movement is obedience. Prayer without action is incomplete. Faith without obedience is ineffective. Revelation without response is wasted.

Action is the bridge between what God says and what God does. It is the believer's active cooperation with Heaven's instruction. God speaks, leads, prompts, convicts, directs, and reveals—but His will is manifested when the believer obeys. Prayer positions the believer to hear; obedience positions them to walk in what they have heard. Jesus said plainly, "If ye love me, keep my commandments."[1] Obedience is the evidence of love, not the substitute for it. It is the response of a heart transformed by fellowship with God, which gives you boldness to act.

Obedience Is the Fruit of Relationship

Obedience is not legalism or religious duty. It is the natural outflow of relationship. When a believer communes deeply with the Father, they begin to desire His will, honor His voice, and trust His leading. Obedience becomes a joy, not a burden. John wrote, "And his commandments are not grievous."[2] Why? Because love transforms obedience from obligation into delight.

The more time believers spend in prayer, the easier obedience becomes. Prayer softens the heart. It tunes the spiritual ear. It cultivates sensitivity. It builds trust. It removes resistance. When prayer is consistent, obedience becomes reflexive. When prayer is neglected, obedience becomes difficult.

God Responds to Obedience

Scripture repeatedly shows that God's blessings are connected to obedience. This does not mean obedience earns God's love—His love is unconditional. But obedience positions the believer to receive what God has already willed to give. Isaiah declares, "If ye be willing and obedient, ye shall eat the good of the land."[3] Willingness opens the heart; obedience opens the door.

When God gives an instruction, He attaches a blessing to it. Breakthrough is often waiting on the other side of obedience. Some believers pray earnestly for answers, yet refuse to follow the simple instructions God has already given. They desire a miracle, yet resist the step that activates the miracle. God works with the obedient, not the idle. He partners with those who respond.

Many of Jesus' miracles required action:

- The man with the withered hand had to stretch out his hand.[4]
- The blind man had to wash in the pool of Siloam.[5]
- The ten lepers had to go show themselves to the priest.[6]
- The servants at Cana had to fill the water pots.[7]
- Peter had to cast his net again despite exhaustion.[8]

In each case, the miracle followed obedience—not before it.

Obedience Turns Prayer Into Movement

Prayers without obedience remain spiritual potential; obedience turns them into spiritual manifestation. A believer may pray for wisdom, but unless they follow the direction God gives, wisdom remains theoretical. A believer may pray for provision, but unless they obey the financial principles God reveals, provision remains limited. A believer may pray for healing in relationships, but unless they obey the command to forgive, healing remains distant.

Obedience activates answers. It unlocks strategies. It converts divine revelation into earthly reality. When believers move, Heaven moves with them.

Actions Requires Faith

Action is rarely comfortable, convenient, or logical. It often requires stepping into the unknown, moving despite uncertainty, and acting without visible security. This is why obedience is an act of faith. The writer of Hebrews declares, "By faith Abraham obeyed."[9] Faith produces obedience, and obedience proves faith.

God often gives instructions that stretch human understanding: *"Leave your country." "Build an ark." "Step into the Jordan." "Speak to the rock." "Feed them yourselves."*

These commands required trust, not clarity. The believer may not always understand the instruction, but they must trust the Instructor. God never requires blind obedience—He requires faith-filled obedience.

Action Must Be Immediate

Delayed action is disobedience. When God speaks, He expects response without hesitation. Not because He demands urgency, but because delay gives room for doubt, fear, and reasoning to interfere.

When God nudges the believer, that nudge is time-sensitive—it is connected to a moment, a window, an opportunity.

When Philip was told by the Spirit to join the chariot, he ran.[10] He did not negotiate or analyze—he responded. That action resulted in the Ethiopian's salvation, which history tells us became the seed of Christianity in Africa.

Immediate action produces immediate impact.

Action Required Even When the Instruction Seems Small

Many of God's instructions appear insignificant. Yet these "small" instructions often become the seeds of major breakthroughs. Naaman nearly missed his healing because the instruction—wash seven times in the Jordan—seemed too simple.[11] The widow nearly missed her miracle because the instruction—pour oil—seemed too small.[12] Peter nearly missed his calling because the instruction—throw your net on the other side—seemed unnecessary.[13]

Small actions produces big results because God attaches supernatural power to natural actions.

Action Requires Surrender

True obedience with action cannot exist without surrender. The believer must relinquish control—the need to understand, the desire to predict, the impulse to manage outcomes. This is the heart of Jesus' prayer in Gethsemane: "Not my will, but thine, be done."[14] Surrender is not weakness; it is trust. It is the recognition that God knows more, sees more, and desires more for His children than they can imagine.

When the believer surrenders, obedience becomes easier. The heart ceases to wrestle. The spirit becomes light. The believer gains peace because they are no longer carrying the burden of figuring everything out. Obedience with action flows naturally from a surrendered heart.

Obedience with Action Produces Transformation

Obedience does not simply change circumstances—it changes people. Every act of obedience shapes the believer's character. It deepens intimacy with God, strengthens spiritual maturity, and refines sensitivity to the Spirit. Obedience is sanctifying. It aligns the believer more fully with the nature of Christ.

Jesus Himself "learned obedience by the things which He suffered."[15] This does not mean Jesus was disobedient and needed correction—it means obedience was tested, proven, and perfected through experience. Likewise, believers grow through obedience, not simply intention.

Action Is Evidence of Hearing God

Jesus declared, "My sheep hear my voice… and they follow me."[16] Hearing and following are inseparable. Many believers want to hear God clearly, yet they do not act on the guidance He has already given. Obedience sharpens spiritual hearing; disobedience dulls it. The more the believer obeys, the easier the next instruction becomes. The Spirit trusts the responsive heart with greater revelation.

Action Opens Doors, Opportunities, and Favor

Throughout Scripture, obedience unlocks divine favor.

- Joseph obeyed in prison and was promoted to the palace.[17]
- Ruth obeyed Naomi and stepped into destiny.[18]
- Joshua obeyed and walls collapsed.[19]
- Gideon obeyed and defeated an army.[20]

Obedience is the key that opens doors no man can shut. It aligns believers with divine timing, supernatural provision, and strategic opportunities. Favor follows obedience.

Conclusion: Prayer That Moves God Requires Actions & Obedience That Moves You

Action and Obedience is the final movement of prayer because it releases the power of prayer into real life. Without obedience, the believer remains inspired but unchanged, informed but inactive, stirred but stagnant. Prayer prepares the heart—obedience activates the plan while action manifest the blessings.

This is why prayer and obedience must remain inseparable. Prayer reveals God's will; obedience fulfills it. Prayer awakens faith; obedience expresses it. Prayer opens Heaven; obedience brings Heaven into the earth and actions brings God closer to you.

Let obedience become your lifestyle. Let surrender become your posture. Let God's voice become your instruction manual. For the believer who obeys will see miracles, breakthroughs, divine favor, and spiritual maturity beyond anything they imagined.

When God speaks, respond. When the Spirit nudges, move. When the Word instructs, act.

For prayer without obedience is incomplete—but prayer with obedience becomes unstoppable. For with God nothing shall be impossible—Luke 1:37

My Mother's Wisdom

My mother used to say, "Nothing comes to a sleeper but a dream—and by the time the sleeper wakes up, the dream is gone." In other words, wake up and move. Go after it.

God will not drag you into your blessing. He will walk *with* you—but not *for* you. GO FOR IT GO GET IT.. ITS YOURS FOR THE ASKING!

Footnotes
1. John 14:15 (KJV)
2. 1 John 5:3 (KJV)
3. Isaiah 1:19 (KJV)
4. Mark 3:5 (KJV)
5. John 9:7 (KJV)
6. Luke 17:14 (KJV)
7. John 2:7 (KJV)
8. Luke 5:4–6 (KJV)
9. Hebrews 11:8 (KJV)
10. Acts 8:29–30 (KJV)
11. 2 Kings 5:10–14 (KJV)
12. 2 Kings 4:1–7 (KJV)
13. John 21:6 (KJV)
14. Luke 22:42 (KJV)
15. Hebrews 5:8 (KJV)
16. John 10:27 (KJV)
17. Genesis 39–41 (KJV)
18. Ruth 3–4 (KJV)
19. Joshua 6:1–20 (KJV)
20. Judges 7:1–22 (KJV)

CONCLUSION

"Draw nigh to God, and he will draw nigh to you." — James 4:8

A Life Shaped by Prayer: From Discipline to Delight, From Routine to Relationship

Prayer is not merely a practice of the Christian life — it is the Christian life. Everything in the believer's walk with God flows from prayer: identity, intimacy, authority, discernment, strength, peace, direction, power, and spiritual transformation. Prayer is the breath of the soul, the language of fellowship, the posture of humility, and the engine of spiritual growth. It is the place where the human heart meets the divine will, where weakness encounters strength, where confusion meets wisdom, where emptiness encounters fullness.

Throughout this book, you have journeyed through seven foundational movements of prayer: worship, repentance, the Word, petition, praying in the Spirit, thanksgiving, and obedience. These are not isolated techniques or mechanical steps—they are a spiritual rhythm. They form a pattern of communion that shapes the believer into the image of Christ and draws them into deeper levels of intimacy with the Father. Together, they teach us not simply how to pray but how to live in continual fellowship with God.

Prayer Begins With Relationship

True prayer is impossible apart from relationship. Jesus opened the model prayer by saying, "Our Father."[1] This is the foundational revelation of all Christian prayer—that we approach God not as a distant deity but as a loving Father. Prayer begins with belonging, not begging. It grows from identity, not insecurity. You pray not to earn God's attention but because you already have it.

When believers understand that God is Father—compassionate, attentive, loving, and present—prayer becomes natural. It becomes the ongoing conversation between the child and the Father, the disciple and the Master, the servant and the Lord, the friend and the Companion. Everything in prayer flows from this relationship.

Prayer Reorients the Heart

Each movement of prayer reshapes the interior world. Worship lifts the eyes of the heart. Repentance purifies the conscience. The Word grounds the mind. Petition builds faith. Praying in the Spirit empowers intercession. Thanksgiving cultivates joy. Obedience activates revelation. In the hands of the Holy Spirit, prayer becomes the tool that reorders every part of a believer's life.

Prayer is not simply an act—it is a reorientation. It turns the heart away from fear toward faith, away from bitterness toward forgiveness, away from anxiety toward peace, away from self-sufficiency toward God-dependence. The more a believer prays, the more they are transformed.

Prayer Is Where Weakness Meets God's Strength

Paul teaches that the Holy Spirit "helpeth our infirmities," because we "know not what we should pray for as we ought."[2] Prayer is not the place of human mastery but of human yielding. It is where weakness becomes the entryway for divine strength. God does not require perfect articulation—He requires surrendered hearts.

When believers come to prayer with their frailty, limitations, questions, and struggles, they meet a God who is not intimidated by weakness but drawn to it. Prayer becomes the place where burdens exchange for strength, confusion for clarity, heaviness for joy, and despair for hope. No believer leaves the presence of God unchanged.

Prayer Positions Us for Transformation

Prayer is not only communication—it is formation. It shapes Christ in the believer. It deepens humility, expands love, strengthens self-control, and cultivates spiritual fruit. The more time one spends with God, the more they resemble Him. Moses' face shone after encountering God.[3] Jesus returned from prayer in the wilderness "in the power of the Spirit."[4] Likewise, believers who consistently pray carry spiritual weight, authority, and clarity.

Prayer transforms the heart privately so that the believer can walk in purpose publicly. It purifies motives, corrects attitudes, strengthens convictions, and awakens compassion. Prayer prepares the believer for every assignment, battle, decision, and opportunity God will bring.

Prayer Aligns Us With the Will of God

Jesus prayed, "Not my will, but Thine be done."[5] This is the greatest prayer of surrender, the highest posture of obedience, and the purest expression of trust. Prayer is not the attempt to bend God toward our desires—it is the act of bending the believer toward God's desires.

When prayer becomes continual, alignment becomes natural. The believer stops striving for their own will and begins seeking God's. They become less reactive and more responsive. They listen more and speak less. They become available for divine assignments. Their desires are purified, their ambitions refined, and their decisions sanctified.

Prayer does not change God—prayer changes the believer until they want what God wants, love what He loves, and surrender to what He ordains.

Prayer Is an Invitation Into Partnership With God

God has chosen to accomplish His will on earth through partnership with His people. Prayer is one of the primary means by which that partnership is activated. When believers intercede, Heaven responds.

When they declare the Word, spiritual atmospheres shift. When they pray in the Spirit, strongholds break. When they pray with faith, miracles unfold.

Scripture reveals a God who listens to the cries of His people, responds to their petitions, and moves through their intercession. Abraham prayed and nations were blessed.[6] Hannah prayed and a prophet was born.[7] Elijah prayed and the rain returned.[8] The church prayed and prison doors opened.[9] God has woven prayer into the fabric of His purposes.

Prayer Without Obedience Leaves Heaven Waiting

As the final chapter demonstrated, obedience is the culmination of prayer. Many believers hear God in prayer but fail to obey Him afterward. Revelation without obedience is interruption. God speaks so that His will may be performed, not merely heard. When believers align their actions with God's instruction, Heaven's purposes manifest on earth.

Some breakthroughs remain unrealized because believers have prayed but not obeyed. They have asked God for direction but refused to take the step. They have sought provision but resisted stewardship. They have asked for healing but resisted forgiveness. They have requested clarity but neglected the Word.

Prayer reveals God's will; obedience releases it.

Prayer Must Become a Lifestyle, Not an Event

The apostle Paul instructed the church to "pray without ceasing."[10] This does not mean praying nonstop but living in a continual state of communion. It means walking with God throughout the day, acknowledging Him in decisions, inviting Him into conversations, seeking His presence in moments of stillness, and listening for His whisper in times of movement.

A lifestyle of prayer transforms daily routines into sacred rhythms. Driving becomes communion. Moments of silence become invitation. Work becomes worship. Difficulties become opportunities to draw near. Prayer becomes the atmosphere of the believer's life.

Prayer Produces Sensitivity to the Holy Spirit

The more believers pray, the more attuned they become to the Spirit's leading. They recognize His nudges, discern His warnings, and respond to His invitations. Prayer sharpens spiritual perception. It teaches believers to distinguish between God's voice, their own impulses, and the enemy's deception.

Many mistakes in life are made because people moved without praying, or prayed but did not listen. But believers who cultivate prayer with listening become guided by the Spirit instead of pushed by circumstances.

Prayer Prepares Us for Spiritual Warfare

Scripture teaches that believers live in a spiritual battle. Prayer is essential for victory. It equips the believer with discernment, sharpens spiritual weapons, and empowers the inner life. Prayer strengthens faith when the enemy attacks, protects the mind from deception, and fortifies the heart against discouragement.

Jesus warned Peter that Satan desired to sift him like wheat, but Jesus prayed for him.[11] Prayer shields believers from what they cannot see and strengthens them for what they must face.

Prayer Is a Privilege and a Responsibility

Prayer is not simply a resource—it is a calling. It is the privilege of meeting with God, but it is also the responsibility of partnering with Him. God has entrusted His people with authority to bind, loose, declare, intercede, and stand in the gap. Prayer changes families, communities, churches, nations, and generations.

Believers must never underestimate the weight of prayer. Heaven moves when the saints pray. Demons tremble when the righteous cry out. Angels are dispatched when faith is activated. Prayer is divine power entrusted to human vessels.

Final Exhortation: Become a Person of Prayer

As you conclude this book, let this truth settle deeply in your spirit: prayer is the pathway to everything God desires to accomplish in your life. It is not optional. It is essential.

Pray when you feel strong. Pray when you feel weak.
Pray when you understand. Pray when you don't.
Pray when God seems near. Pray when He seems silent.
Pray when you are certain. Pray when you are confused.
Pray in the morning, pray throughout the day, pray before you sleep.

Make prayer your habitation — not your emergency room.

Become a worshiper.
Remain repentant.
Stay rooted in the Word.
Ask boldly.
Pray in the Spirit.
Give thanks continually.
Obey immediately.

And you will discover that prayer is not merely a discipline—it is a relationship, a joy, a refuge, and a source of unending strength.

May the Holy Spirit take these teachings and engrave them into your heart, expanding your prayer life, deepening your communion, and empowering you to walk in the fullness of fellowship with your Father.

May you become not only a person who prays, but a person whose life is prayer.

Footnotes

1. Matthew 6:9 (KJV)
2. Romans 8:26 (KJV)
3. Exodus 34:29–35 (KJV)
4. Luke 4:14 (KJV)
5. Luke 22:42 (KJV)
6. Genesis 18:22–33 (KJV)
7. 1 Samuel 1:10–20 (KJV)
8. 1 Kings 18:41–45 (KJV)
9. Acts 12:5–11 (KJV)
10. 1 Thessalonians 5:17 (KJV)
11. Luke 22:31–32 (KJV)

TEACH US HOW TO PRAY

APPENDIX A
STUDY GUIDE

Step-by-Step Reflection and Practice

This study guide is designed to help individuals, small groups, and congregations apply the principles of prayer in a practical and transformative way. Each section includes a summary, key Scriptures, reflection prompts, and actionable steps.

Step 1 — WORSHIP

Summary

Worship is the divine doorway into God's presence. It orients the heart toward God's greatness, goodness, and holiness. Prayer begins with worship because worship aligns the soul with Heaven before any request is made.

Key Scriptures

Psalm 100:4; Exodus 3:5; Matthew 6:9

Reflection

- How has your understanding of worship changed after reading this chapter?
- Do you tend to rush into prayer without worship? Why?

Practice

Spend 5–10 minutes worshiping God daily using Scripture, songs, or personal expressions.

Step 2 — REPENTANCE

Summary

Repentance is the cleansing of the heart, removing spiritual barriers and restoring intimacy. It brings forgiveness, freedom, and renewed fellowship with God.

Key Scriptures

Psalm 51; 1 John 1:9; Isaiah 59:2

Reflection

- What areas of your life require repentance?
- Why is repentance essential before petition?

Practice

Pray Psalm 139:23–24 daily, inviting the Holy Spirit to search your heart.

Step 3 — THE WORD

Summary

The Word of God anchors prayer in truth, shapes desires, builds faith, and strengthens spiritual authority.

Key Scriptures

Isaiah 55:11; Hebrews 4:12; John 15:7

Reflection

- How does Scripture influence your prayers?
- Which Scriptures do you rely on during spiritual battles?

Practice

Choose one Scripture daily to pray aloud and meditate on.

Step 4 — PETITION

Summary

Petition is the act of asking God boldly and confidently, standing on His promises and trusting His nature.

Key Scriptures

Mark 11:24; 1 John 5:14; Philippians 4:6

Reflection

- Do you ask God boldly or timidly?
- How can your petitions become more aligned with God's will?

Practice

Write 3 specific petitions and pray them daily with Scripture support.

Step 5 — PRAYING IN THE SPIRIT

Summary

Praying in the Spirit empowers believers to pray beyond their understanding and partner with the Holy Spirit in supernatural intercession.

Key Scriptures

Romans 8:26–27; Jude 20; 1 Corinthians 14:14–15

Reflection

- What limits your willingness to pray in the Spirit?
- How has praying in tongues strengthened your faith?

Practice

Set aside 10 minutes of uninterrupted time each day to pray in the Spirit.

Step 6 — THANKSGIVING

Summary

Thanksgiving is the posture that honors God, strengthens faith, promotes peace, and guards the heart from heaviness.

Key Scriptures

1 Thessalonians 5:18; Psalm 107:1; Philippians 4:6–7

Reflection

- What has God done for you that you have not thanked Him for recently?
- How does gratitude shift your emotional and spiritual atmosphere?

Practice

Create a gratitude journal and list 3 things daily.

Step 7 — ACTION (OBEDIENCE)

Summary

Obedience completes prayer. It activates divine instruction and positions the believer for blessing, breakthrough, and transformation.

Key Scriptures

John 14:15; Isaiah 1:19; James 1:22

Reflection

- What instructions has God given you that you have delayed?
- How does obedience increase spiritual clarity?

Practice

Identify one divine instruction you have not acted on — and obey it this week.

APPENDIX B
DISCUSSION QUESTIONS

Step 1 — WORSHIP

1. How does beginning prayer with worship shift your mindset and spiritual posture before you speak a single request?
2. What is the difference between saying words of praise and entering true worship from the heart?
3. Reflect on a moment when God's presence became noticeably tangible during worship. What led to that experience?
4. Why do you believe God requires worship as the first movement in prayer? What does it reveal about His nature?
5. How can you cultivate a lifestyle of worship that continues outside of your prayer time?

Step 2 — REPENTANCE

1. What emotions or internal responses arise when you approach God in repentance? Are they healthy or fear-based?
2. How does repentance restore intimacy and remove spiritual blockages between you and God?
3. In what ways does repentance reorient your desires and purify your motives for prayer?
4. How can believers practice ongoing repentance without falling into condemnation or shame?
5. Is there an area where God has been convicting you recently? What steps will you take to respond?

Step 3 — THE WORD

1. How does incorporating Scripture into prayer shift the authority and confidence with which you pray?

2. What Scriptures have become foundational to your life? How do they influence how you approach God?
3. How can believers guard against praying outside of God's will by anchoring their petitions in His Word?
4. Discuss a time when a single verse or passage reshaped your perspective or brought breakthrough.
5. How can you increase your intake and meditation on the Word to strengthen your prayer life?

Step 4 — PETITION

1. What keeps many believers from asking boldly in prayer, and how can Scripture correct those limitations?
2. How do you personally determine whether a request aligns with God's will?
3. Why is specificity important in petition? How does vague prayer weaken spiritual authority?
4. Share an example of a petition God answered clearly. What did you learn about His character?
5. What petitions are you currently bringing before God, and what Scriptures support those requests?

Step 5 — PRAYING IN THE SPIRIT

1. What differences do you notice when you pray in the Spirit compared to praying with your natural understanding?
2. Why is praying in tongues a powerful tool for spiritual warfare, clarity, and strengthening the inner man?
3. How can believers overcome hesitation, fear, or confusion about praying in the Spirit?
4. Discuss a moment when praying in the Spirit brought breakthrough, peace, or revelation.
5. What practical habits can you implement to cultivate a consistent life of praying in the Spirit?

Step 6 — THANKSGIVING

1. How does thanksgiving transform your emotional and spiritual atmosphere during prayer?
2. Why is gratitude considered a spiritual weapon against heaviness, discouragement, and anxiety?
3. Reflect on a past season in which thanksgiving carried you through difficulty. What did it teach you?
4. How can believers ensure that gratitude becomes a lifestyle instead of a reaction to blessings?
5. What blessings, big or small, have you recently overlooked—and how will you give thanks for them now?

Step 7 — ACTION (OBEDIENCE)

1. What is the connection between hearing God in prayer and obeying Him afterward? Why is obedience essential?
2. Describe a time when delayed obedience caused unnecessary struggle or missed opportunity.
3. Why does God often attach breakthrough, favor, or provision to specific acts of obedience?
4. How can believers cultivate a heart that responds quickly and joyfully to God's instructions?
5. What is one instruction God has given you recently that you need to act upon—and when will you do it?

APPENDIX C
GLOSSARY OF PRAYER TERMS

A Comprehensive Guide to Language, Concepts, and Practices of a Biblical Prayer Life

Abiding

Staying continually connected to God through prayer, obedience, and spiritual attentiveness. Abiding represents a relational nearness where the believer remains aware of God's presence, aligned with His Word, and responsive to His voice. Jesus taught that fruitfulness flows from abiding (John 15).

Adoration

A form of worship that expresses deep love, reverence, and affection toward God. Adoration focuses entirely on who God is—His character, holiness, wisdom, power, and beauty—rather than on His gifts. It softens the heart and lifts the believer's gaze upward.

Alignment

A spiritual condition in which one's desires, thoughts, motives, and actions come into agreement with God's will. Alignment is essential for powerful prayer because it positions the believer to request what God has already purposed to accomplish.

Authority (Spiritual)

The delegated power God gives believers to speak, act, and pray in His name. Spiritual authority is exercised through righteousness, faith, obedience, and revelation of identity. It allows the believer to resist the enemy, declare God's Word, and influence spiritual atmospheres.

Binding and Loosing

A biblical concept referring to the believer's authority to forbid or permit spiritual activity in agreement with Heaven (Matthew 16:19).

- Binding: Restricting or prohibiting demonic influence or activity.
- Loosing: Releasing God's power, favor, angelic assistance, or blessings.

Confession

Acknowledging sin openly before God with humility and sincerity. Confession restores fellowship and softens the heart. It is the first act of repentance and aligns the believer with truth.

Consecration

Setting oneself apart for God's purposes through purity, dedication, and focused devotion. Consecration prepares the believer for deeper levels of prayer and spiritual effectiveness.

Covenant Prayer

Prayer based on the promises, principles, and provisions God has established through covenant. Covenant prayer is confident because it stands on what God has already said.

Discernment

The Spirit-enabled ability to distinguish between truth and deception, divine leading and human desire, or godly influence and demonic interference. Discernment is vital for accurate praying and decision-making.

Devotion

Daily acts of prayer, worship, Scripture reading, and fellowship with God that strengthen intimacy. Devotion cultivates consistency and spiritual sensitivity.

Edification

The building up of the inner person through prayer, Scripture, worship, and spiritual disciplines. Praying in the Spirit particularly produces edification (Jude 20).

Fasting

The voluntary abstaining from food or certain pleasures to seek God more deeply, heighten spiritual sensitivity, weaken the flesh, and strengthen the spirit. Fasting amplifies prayer and breaks spiritual resistance.

Fellowship (Koinonia)

Deep relational communion with God and other believers. It involves shared participation in spiritual life, prayer, worship, and mutual encouragement.

Hearing God

The ability to perceive the Lord's voice through Scripture, the Holy Spirit, prayer, inner promptings, wise counsel, and divine impressions. Hearing God is developed through consistent intimacy and obedience.

Impartation

A spiritual transfer of grace, gifting, power, or revelation through prayer, laying on of hands, or divine encounter. Impartation often strengthens or activates spiritual gifts.

Intercession

Praying on behalf of another person, group, church, or nation. Intercession involves standing in the gap, carrying spiritual burdens, and partnering with God to bring His will into the earth.

Meditation (Biblical)
Focusing the mind and heart on Scripture, turning it over repeatedly, absorbing its truths, and allowing the Spirit to illuminate meaning. Meditation strengthens faith and renews the mind.

Obedience
Responding to God's voice with action. Obedience completes the cycle of prayer and unlocks divine blessing. It is the fruit of surrender and love.

Petition
Directly presenting needs, desires, and requests to God based on His promises and character. Petition must be specific, faith-filled, and aligned with His will.

Praise
Verbal or expressive celebration of God's goodness, acts, and faithfulness. Praise uplifts the believer's spirit and shifts spiritual atmospheres.

Prayer of Agreement
When two or more believers unite in prayer for the same request, standing in unity and faith (Matthew 18:19). Agreement amplifies spiritual authority.

Prayer of Consecration
A prayer of surrender in which the believer commits their will to God's will ("Not my will, but Thine be done").

Prayer of Faith
A confident prayer rooted in the promises of God and spoken without wavering. The prayer of faith expects results because it stands on God's integrity.

Prayer Mantle

A spiritual calling or grace to intercede, war, or lead others in prayer. A mantle is often accompanied by spiritual authority and emotional burden for prayer.

Praying in the Spirit

Prayer inspired, empowered, and directed by the Holy Ghost, often expressed through tongues. This type of prayer bypasses human intellect and aligns the believer with divine will.

Prophetic Intercession

Prayer that flows from the Spirit's revelation, where believers intercede for future events, hidden matters, or divine assignments. Prophetic intercession partners with Heaven's agenda.

Repentance

A change of mind and direction away from sin and toward God. Repentance cleanses, restores, and reopens spiritual communication.

Reverence

A holy respect for God's presence, majesty, and holiness. Reverence is the foundation of worship and the beginning of wisdom.

Sacrifice of Praise

Worship offered during difficulty or emotional struggle. It is the act of praising God despite circumstances and is deeply pleasing to Him (Hebrews 13:15).

Sanctification

The process by which the Holy Spirit purifies the believer's heart, transforms their character, and conforms them to Christ's image. Prayer accelerates sanctification.

Spiritual Authority

The believer's God-given right to pray, declare, bind, loose, resist the enemy, and enforce the victory of Christ through prayer and obedience.

Spiritual Burden

A weight or urgency placed on the believer's heart by the Holy Spirit to pray, intercede, or stand in the gap for a person, situation, or territory.

Spiritual Warfare

Engaging in prayer against demonic forces, lies, strongholds, and satanic assignments. Warfare prayer is driven by Scripture, the name of Jesus, and the authority of the Spirit.

Strongholds

Patterns of thinking or spiritual structures that resist God's truth. They are dismantled through Scripture, repentance, and spiritual warfare (2 Corinthians 10:4–5).

Supplication

Earnest, heartfelt pleading before God for personal or urgent needs. Supplication reveals humility and dependence.

Thanksgiving

Expressing gratitude to God for His goodness, mercy, and provision. Thanksgiving shifts atmosphere, increases faith, and releases peace.

Tongues (Glossolalia)

A supernatural prayer language given by the Holy Spirit that allows believers to pray mysteries, intercede accurately, and edify themselves spiritually.

Warfare Tongues

An intensified flow of praying in the Spirit where the believer engages in spiritual battle, pushing back darkness and breaking resistance.

Watchman Ministry

A calling to spiritually "watch," discern, and intercede for the protection of churches, families, cities, or nations. Watchmen sense threats and pray proactively.

Worship

Responding to God's worth through adoration, awe, surrender, and affection. Worship prepares the heart for communion and draws the believer into intimacy.

Yielding

The act of surrendering personal will, desires, or plans in favor of God's direction. Yielding is essential for Spirit-led prayer.

About the Author

DR. LEON W. CRAWFORD, JR. is a passionate man of God with a heart for people. Called and anointed to reach individuals from all walks of life—especially youth and those unfamiliar with Jesus—his ministry has led many to salvation and renewed faith.

In 1997, he founded his ministry in Inkster, MI, with just seven members and a mission to show Christ through action. From delivering food in the "Saigon Projects" to forming community programs, Dr. Crawford has consistently prioritized outreach over tradition, living out his vision: "ROAR: Relationships Over All Religion."

Under his direction, Citi Praise Church has developed a non-profit organization called GET-A-LIFE, Inc. Through this non-profit Dr. Crawford has made a significant impact on the youth in the community by founding the Boys 2 Men summer program- an initiative focused on mentoring young men by teaching them practical life skills. Outreach is said to be one the most fulfilling aspects of ministry for him.

Educated at Wilberforce University, Logos Bible College, and St. Thomas Christian College (Doctorate, Hon.), Dr. Crawford is committed to raising up disciples who disciple others. Dr. Crawford has been mentored by many great people of God, such as Apostle Ken Hubbard, Bishop H.L. Jackson, Bishop Milton Jackson, Bishop Wayne T. Jackson, along with his Praying Grandmother "Mother" Willie May Lewis just to name a few.

As a third-generation preacher, Pastor Crawford has learned the revelation and truth in God's Word. Dr. Crawford believes it's time to present "CHRIST in the COMMUNITY with a hands-on approach with Christians living a BALANCED LIFESTYLE. He is a devoted husband, father of five, and proud grandfather. Dr. Crawford lives by Romans 4:21—*Being fully persuaded that what He had promised, He was able also to perform.*" A trailblazer and non-traditional voice in ministry, he is devoted to rebuilding cities and transforming lives through the love of Jesus Christ.

www.ingramcontent.com/pod-product-compliance
Lightning Source LLC
Chambersburg PA
CBHW051223120626
46547CB00013B/1484